The Future of Europe

In 2004 the European Union's Intergovernmental Conference finalises the historic process of enlarging the European Union from fifteen to twenty-five members. This book is the most detailed and up-to-date account of the state of the European Union on the eve of its biggest enlargement so far and also considers its future prospects in several key areas. The book explains why the ten applicant countries wanted to join and how they succeeded after lengthy negotiations.

Each chapter gives a cutting-edge overview by a leading figure in the field and subjects covered include:

- the enlargement–integration debate
- the politics of the European Union's new member states
- the role of the European Convention
- the political economy of an enlarged Europe
- the challenges of developing common European foreign and security policy
- the European Union's relations with its neighbours
- EU–American relations

With an analysis of US attitudes towards a new enlarged Europe, this state-of-the-art summary of the Eropean Union is essential reading for students of European politics and European Studies at a key moment in the European Union's history.

Fraser Cameron is Director of Studies at the European Policy Centre in Brussels. A former academic and diplomat, he was a foreign policy advisor in the European Commission from 1990–2002, serving 1999–2001 in the EU delegation in Washington, DC.

The Future of Europe

Integration and enlargement

Edited by Fraser Cameron

Routledge
Taylor & Francis Group

LONDON AND NEW YORK

First published 2004
by Routledge
11 New Fetter Lane, London EC4P 4EE

Simultaneously published in the USA and Canada
by Routledge
29 West 35th Street, New York, NY 10001

Routledge is an imprint of the Taylor & Francis Group

© 2004 Fraser Cameron for selection and editorial matter;
individual chapters, the contributors

Typeset in Sabon by Exe Valley Dataset Ltd, Exeter
Printed and bound in Great Britain by
The Cromwell Press, Trowbridge, Wiltshire

All rights reserved. No part of this book may be reprinted or
reproduced or utilised in any form or by any electronic, mechanical,
or other means, now known or hereafter invented, including
photocopying and recording, or in any information storage or
retrieval system, without permission in writing from the publishers.

British Library Cataloguing in Publication Data
A catalogue record for this book is available from the British Library

Library of Congress Cataloging in Publication Data
The future of Europe: integration and enlargement / edited by Fraser Cameron.
    p. cm.
   1. European Union.   2. Security, International.   3. European federation.
   4. European union–Membership.   5. Europe–Economic integration.
   6. European Union countries–Politics and government.   7. European Union
   countries–Economic policy.   I. Cameron, Fraser, 1947–

JN30.F83 2004
341.242´2–dc22   2003017195

ISBN 0–415–32483–1 (hbk)
ISBN 0–415–32484–X (pbk)

Contents

Figures and tables

Figures

Tables

Contributors

David Allen is Professor and Head of Department of European and International Studies, Loughborough University, UK.

Graham Avery is Chief Advisor in DG Enlargement of the European Commission, Brussels. (He writes here in a personal capacity.)

Fraser Cameron (editor) is Director of Studies, the European Policy Centre, Brussels.

Heather Grabbe is Deputy Director of the Centre for European Reform (CER), London, and non-stipendiary Fellow of Wolfson College, Oxford.

Geoffrey Harris is Head of Division for Interparliamentary Relations (Enlargement), the European Parliament, Brussels.

Antonio Missiroli is Senior Research Fellow, the EU Institute of Security Studies, Paris.

Gerrard Quille is Deputy Director of International Security Information Service (ISIS), Europe, Brussels.

Andrew Scott is Professor of Economics and Director of the Europa Institute, Edinburgh University, UK.

Simon Serfaty holds the Zbigniew Brzezinski Chair in Global Security and Geostrategy and is Director of the Europe Programme, the Centre for International and Strategic Studies (CSIS), Washington, DC.

Foreword

We are not always aware that we are living through major historical changes. It is usually some time before we realise what we have seen. Occasionally, however, history crystallises into a single overwhelming event. We have all witnessed such an historical event in 2003. In April, in Athens, 25 heads of state and government signed the most comprehensive and politically most far-reaching Accession Treaty in the history of European integration. There was no alternative to this enlargement for both political and economic reasons. It finally brings to an end the division of Europe, which resulted from the tragic history of our continent in the twentieth century.

Looking back over the history of European integration, it is striking that the great enterprise was primarily motivated by a desire for peace. The concept of peace through integration runs like a leitmotif through the sometimes impenetrable integration process. Today, the political and economic fabric of Europe is so tightly woven that the countries involved are inextricably dependent on each other and share a common destiny.

The two aspects of European integration, deepening and widening, do not contradict each other. At this stage of the EU's development, further integration and enlarging of the Union are taking place simultaneously. This is a great challenge, but there is no alternative. The European Union has made enormous progress due to the unique tool it has developed: the Community method. If Europe wants to claim its role as a global player, it must continue to pursue its integration process including in key areas such as economic, monetary and social policy.

The European Union is currently reviewing its framework of primary law. For the first time in its history a Convention composed of representatives of the European Parliament, the national parliaments and the governments of the member states of the enlarged Union has convened and prepared a draft constitution that will ensure the functioning of the enlarged Union in the future.

Europe is not a global power, but a global player. It is by far the biggest single donor in international development policy. The Union is spearheading the implementation of global environmental objectives. Europe is the world's strongest trading partner and has gone further than any other bloc in opening its markets to the world's poorest countries. It also has much experience with bringing stability and democracy to countries which need stable and reliable partners. Europe now needs to translate these achievements into an effective European contribution to global governance. At the same time, Europe needs a stable and viable relationship with the United States, based on a common geopolitical agenda.

Many of these issues are discussed in greater detail in this book. *The Future of Europe: Integration and Enlargement*, edited by Fraser Cameron with contributions by authors well known in the academic and policy worlds, is worthwhile reading. I can only invite you to take a closer look.

Guenter Verheugen
European Commission
July 2003

Preface

The future of Europe is the subject of many conferences, seminars, lectures and essays. Will the European Union (EU) become a federal state? What are the boundaries of Europe? How will enlargement impact on the institutions of the Union? What will be the economic impact of enlargement? Will the enlarged Union be able to play a greater role on the world stage? How will the United States (US) view the enlarged EU? As this book makes clear, there are no simple answers to these questions. The EU is heading at speed into the unknown. The domestic and international environments in which the Union will have to operate are becoming less stable. The collapse of communism led to a bloody war in the Balkans and a proliferation of new states in Europe. Six of the states that will join the EU in May 2004 did not even exist 15 years ago. Terrorism and transnational crime have moved up the agenda but many Europeans are more concerned about unemployment or pensions that lose their value.

As the Union faced its fifth and most challenging enlargement, it prepared for this momentous event by establishing a Convention on the future of Europe. The draft constitutional treaty agreed by the Convention in July 2003 was the basis for discussions at the intergovernmental conference (IGC) that started in October 2003. The IGC was due to agree a new constitution for the Union before the ten accession states joined in May and before the elections to the European Parliament (EP) in June 2004.

This book seeks to analyse the state of the Union on the eve of these historic changes. After an introductory chapter by the editor reviewing the history of widening and deepening, David Allen explains the background to the Convention, its proceedings and assesses its outcome. The lengthy and difficult enlargement negotiations are covered by Graham Avery, while Heather Grabbe assesses what kind of new member states we are likely to see in the enlarged EU. Andrew Scott examines the economics of the enlarged Union and Geoffrey Harris considers relations between the EU and its neighbours in the Wider Europe. Antonio Missiroli and Gerrard Quille review the security implications of the enlarged EU while Simon Serfaty charts US attitudes towards integration and enlargement. A final chapter by the editor seeks to pull the main themes together and highlight some future trends.

A number of my colleagues at the European Policy Centre, Stanley Crossick, Giovanni Grevi and Guillaume Durrand provided comments on various chapters as did Marek Grela, the Polish ambassador to the EU, Pavel Telicka, his Czech colleague, Kees van Rij and John Wyles. Graham Avery provided useful comments on a number of chapters.

I am especially grateful to Commissioner Guenter Verheugen for writing the foreword to this book. He has successfully overseen the biggest enlargement in the Union's history and, for many years, has been a tireless campaigner for closer integration.

My wife, Margaret, helped with the proof reading and was a source of much support. In thanking my fellow authors, I acknowledge that any errors are my responsibility.

Fraser Cameron
Brussels, July 2003

Abbreviations

CAP	Common Agricultural Policy
CARDS	Community Assistance for Reconstruction, Development and Stabilisation
CEECs	Central and Eastern European Countries
CEFTA	Central European Free Trade Area
CFSP	Common Foreign and Security Policy
COREPER	Committee of Permanent Representatives
EC	European Community/Communities
ECAP	European Capability Action Plan
ECB	European Central Bank
ECJ	European Court of Justice
ECSC	European Coal and Steel Community
EDC	European Defence Community
EEA	European Economic Area
EEC	European Economic Community
EFTA	European Free Trade Association
EMU	European Monetary Union
EP	European Parliament
EPC	European Political Cooperation
ESDP	European Security and Defence Policy
EU	European Union
EUMC	European Union Military Committee
EUMS	European Union Military Staff
EUPM	European Union Police Mission
HHG	Helsinki Headline Goal
ICC	International Criminal Court
ICTY	International Criminal Tribunal for Yugoslavia
IGC	Intergovernmental Conference
IPTF	International Police Task Force
JHA	Justice and Home Affairs
MEDA	Mediterranean Assistance Programme
NATO	North Atlantic Treaty Organization
OSCE	Organisation for Security and Cooperation in Europe

PHARE	Poland and Hungary Assistance for Economic Recovery Programme
PSC	Political and Security Committee
RRF	Rapid Reaction Force
SEA	Single European Act
SHAPE	Supreme Headquarters Allied Powers Europe
TACIS	Technical Assistance for the Commonwealth of Independent States
TEU	Treaty on European Union (Maastricht Treaty)
WEU	Western European Union

1 Widening and deepening

Fraser Cameron

Summary

This chapter reviews the widening–deepening debate that has been a permanent feature of the European Union (EU) since its foundation. It discusses how each previous enlargement has been accompanied by a parallel deepening of the EU. There is a brief description and analysis of the impact of the Convention and enlargement on the functioning of the EU institutions in order to highlight the debates over governance, legitimacy, identity and democratic accountability. It concludes by suggesting that there may be different speeds of integration in an enlarged Union.

Introduction

The EU has progressed since its creation in 1958 through a mixture of widening and deepening, in other words it has taken steps towards closer integration at the same time as it has enlarged. There have been four previous enlargements; in 1973 Britain, Ireland and Denmark joined; in 1981 Greece; in 1986 Spain and Portugal; and in 1995 Austria, Sweden and Finland. In the past 30 years the EU has thus grown from six members with a population of 185 million to 15 members with a population of 375 million. It is now on the eve of its fifth enlargement, from 15 to 25 members with 450 million citizens. This enlargement is the most ambitious project the EU has ever undertaken. It is, in effect, the reunification of the European continent, divided in 1945 after the Second World War, and extends to central and eastern Europe the zone of peace, stability and prosperity that west Europeans have enjoyed for over forty years.

Each round of enlargement has been accompanied by moves forward in the process of integration. The first enlargement led to the EU adopting a regional policy and was preceded by a common fisheries policy. The second and third enlargements led to the single market, a stronger social policy, an increased commitment to solidarity with the poorer regions and greater powers for the European Parliament. The fourth enlargement followed moves towards economic and monetary union and new policy areas in foreign policy and justice and home affairs. Prior to its fifth and biggest enlargement, the Union introduced the single currency (the euro) and is poised to adopt a new constitution that would mark a significant step forward in the process of integration.

This latest enlargement takes place at a time when the EU faces major challenges concerning its democratic legitimacy, its internal cohesion and efficiency, its economic performance and its external role. These issues along with questions of identity, governance and legitimacy were at the heart of the Convention on the future of Europe. On the eve of this momentous leap forward, adopting a new constitution and enlargement, it is useful to review how the integration and enlargement debates and decisions have developed over the years.

The early years

The history of the EU is one of constant change and treaty reforms, driven largely by the related needs for deeper integration and institutional adaptation. When the process of European integration began in the 1950s there were just six countries involved. France, Germany (then West Germany), Italy, Belgium, the Netherlands and Luxembourg formed the European Coal and Steel Community (ECSC) in 1951 and in 1957 the same six countries signed the Treaty of Rome establishing the European Economic Community (EEC), known more usually as the European Community (EC).

The 'founding fathers', statesmen such as Robert Schuman, Konrad Adenauer, Alcide de Gasperi and Jean Monnet, represented war-torn European countries and had the vision to reject the traditional balance of power politics in favour of a new system of shared sovereignty. Symbolically, the first area chosen for European integration was coal and steel, the traditional heavy industries necessary for any war machine. The ECSC provided for a supranational High Authority that took decisions by qualified majority vote (QMV), the essence of the 'community' system of governance. These six founding member states shared a common vision of a European project of integration that would lead to 'an ever closer union' between their peoples and states. Although they never agreed on the final goals of integration (the *finalité politique*), they nevertheless agreed to be bound together in a 'journey to an unknown destination' (Shonfield 1974).

The UK had refused to join the ECSC because of its concerns about sharing sovereignty and again spurned the offer to join the EC. The British government was not only concerned about the supranational aspects of the EC but also sceptical as to whether the project would succeed. The original six founding members proceeded to confound the British doubters by moving steadily forward along the integration path. The EC established a customs union and began to develop common policies in fields such as agriculture and trade.

The first enlargement (UK, Ireland and Denmark) 1973

When the UK changed its mind about the EC and applied to join in 1961 there were concerns in the original six member states as to whether the addition of the UK, with its strong ties to the United States and the Commonwealth, would undermine the drive towards 'an ever closer union'. The French President, Charles de Gaulle, had little sympathy for closer integration, but he had even less sympathy for the UK challenging France's supremacy in the EC. He twice vetoed British membership in 1963 and 1967, citing the UK's close relations with the US as one reason why it was not fit to join in the European enterprise.

The departure of General de Gaulle from office in 1968 opened up a new political perspective. Accession negotiations started in 1971 and Britain joined the EEC on 1 January 1973. Denmark and Ireland, two strongly agricultural countries heavily dependent on the British market, also joined on the same date. The British had helped to establish the rival European Free Trade Association (EFTA) in 1958 with Finland, Sweden, Norway, Denmark, Austria, Switzerland, Iceland and Liechtenstein as members. But EFTA lacked the economic clout and the ambitions of the EC to play a political role and the UK soon concluded that its best interests lay in membership of the EC.

There was considerable optimism amongst many in the original six member states that British membership would lead to more democracy, more openness and more common policies. The double French veto and lengthy waiting period, however, had left considerable resentment and 'Europe' was to become a recurrent sore that would affect British politics for the next thirty years, splitting parties and causing the downfall of several political leaders (Young 1999). When Edward Heath, prime minister during the accession negotiations, lost the 1974 election, the first priority of the new Labour government was to renegotiate the terms of entry. Some slight modifications were achieved allowing the government under prime minister Harold Wilson to win a referendum (65–35 per cent) on the changed terms in 1975. It was suggested later that the voters in Britain, Denmark and Ireland had not been told that they were joining a Community with political aims. The arguments over this first enlargement from six to nine not only soured the general atmosphere but were also to be replayed many times in the next three decades. The basic problem for the UK was that it had declined to join the original club and was thus unable to help shape the rules before 1973.

The first enlargement of the EC was accompanied by significant deepening. A regional policy was created, which initially comprised just 5 per cent of the EU budget but which grew steadily in later years. A common fisheries policy was established, controversially just before the UK joined. There were increased powers for the European Parliament and in 1979 there were the first direct elections to the EP. A Court of Auditors was also established.

The second and third enlargements (Greece, Spain and Portugal) 1981/1986

Although Greece joined the EC (1981) before Spain and Portugal (1986) it is convenient to place them together, as the motives for all three countries joining the Union were similar and together they represented a 'southern' enlargement. They had all thrown off several years of dictatorship and were keen that their new democracies be cemented in the EC. They were all relatively poor countries compared to the EC average and recognised that access to a larger market, combined with generous regional aid, would be powerful spurs to economic reform and growth. The three states also had large agricultural interests and their accession to the Union shifted the balance in favour of those seeking high expenditure in this area. Unlike the central European countries they had basically capitalist-style economic systems, even if there were many areas of protection. In the case of Greece, the European Commission had doubts as to whether it was ready for the rigours of EC membership and proposed a period of preparation before accession but this idea was swept aside by the European Council led by French president Giscard d'Estaing who played an influential role in pushing Greek membership. Political reasons were thus to the fore in the EU taking in these southern new members.

All three states have become very strong proponents of closer integration, albeit on their terms. Greece was an awkward member state for many years because of its troubled relationship with Turkey, now much improved. Spain was a strong champion of regional aid and later, of the structural funds, while Portugal was usually content to hide behind Madrid in fighting these battles. Ireland, a relatively poor and predominantly agricultural country when it joined, often found itself in the 'southern camp' when it came to fighting for increased regional subsidies.

This southern enlargement was also accompanied by deepening. The Single European Act (SEA) of 1987 was the first major treaty reform since 1957 and prepared the ground for completion of the single market in 1992. The heads of state and government met in the format of an intergovernmental conference to negotiate the new treaty. The SEA introduced the principle of cohesion and included two significant institutional changes: greater use of QMV in order to ensure policy output and greater involvement of the EP in legislative and other decision-making procedures, in order to strengthen the EC's democratic legitimacy. The SEA also put on a treaty basis the procedures for European Political Cooperation (EPC) in the field of foreign policy. It also agreed new policies with regard to the environment, economic and social cohesion, research, technology and social affairs. In light of subsequent Conservative Party policy, it is worth noting that Mrs Thatcher was quite content to sign up to this highly significant deepening of the integration process.

Prior to the fourth enlargement, there was a further important step forward in the integration process. The Treaty on European Union (TEU), signed in Maastricht in February 1992, provided for a new name. The member states agreed to establish a European Union (EU) that incorporated the EC and ECSC. The TEU included provisions for Economic and Monetary Union (with a clear timetable for the introduction of the euro), subsidiarity (taking decisions at the lowest possible level), EU citizenship (complementary to national citizenship), the establishment of a common foreign and security policy (CFSP) and closer cooperation on justice and home affairs (JHA). It also established a Committee of the Regions with an advisory role. The treaty also established a complicated 'pillar system' whereby most decisions in the new areas of Union competence were taken by the intergovernmental as opposed to the community system. Furthermore, the TEU marked the first officially sanctioned moves towards a multi-speed Union. The UK negotiated 'opt outs' from the provisions on the euro, the Social Charter that set minimum standards for workers' rights and later refused to join the passport-free area known as Schengen. Prime Minister John Major returned from Maastricht claiming 'game, set and match' to the UK. After the failure of the first referendum to ratify the TEU in June 2002, Denmark also obtained a number of opt outs in the defence and JHA areas.

The Danish 'no' also effectively ended the debate on institutional reform that the then Commission President, Jacques Delors, sought to promote prior to the EU's enlargement to a number of EFTA countries. Delors had argued that even enlarging from 12 to 15 would necessitate a far greater use of QMV in order for the Union to function efficiently. Given the deep disagreements over Maastricht, it was decided to hold another IGC in 1996 to review the operation of the TEU and in particular CFSP. It is worth noting that the 1991 IGC that led to the Treaty of Maastricht was preceded by a meeting of national parliamentarians in Rome. This 'mini Convention' only lasted a week and failed to produce any agreed recommendations to the IGC.

The fourth enlargement (Sweden, Finland and Austria) 1995

The end of the Cold War introduced a new driver of treaty reform: the prospect of enlargement on an unprecedented scale. The first round of post-Cold War enlargement took place in January 1995 when Austria, Finland and Sweden joined the EU. These three states (along with Norway that, for a second time, also negotiated entry but failed to secure ratification in a referendum) had all belonged to EFTA and the new European Economic Area (EEA). Their motives for joining included a lessening of the importance of neutrality after the end of the Cold War and the desire to be at the top table when major political, security and economic issues were being discussed and decided. They were all prosperous states with an average GDP considerably above the EU's average. They already had much experience of intergovernmental cooperation but the community system was new. Finland proved to be the most favourable to the community system, Sweden the least favourable.

With the accession of three new member states, many thought that the EU's decision-making procedures were likely to become even more cumbersome. Accordingly, the EP threatened in 1994, during ratification of the accession agreements, to block enlargement (by means of withholding parliamentary assent) unless the member states agreed to negotiate institutional reforms in a new IGC. The submission of membership applications by a host of central and eastern European countries in the mid-1990s strengthened the case for institutional reform before further enlargement. Specifically, the debate about reform covered the size and composition of the European Commission, the extent and modalities of QMV and how to facilitate closer cooperation among more integration-minded member states.

The 1996 IGC was preceded by a Reflection Group under the chairmanship of Carlos Westendorp, a Spanish diplomat. It was given a wide mandate to review institutional issues but its work was severely handicapped by the obstructionist attitude of John Major's Conservative government in the UK. On issue after issue there were 14 member states in favour and one against. The UK position may, however, have allowed some member states to hide behind the eurosceptic British delegation.

The arrival of the Labour government in the UK in May 1997 was too late to lead to a decisive change in the British approach at the Amsterdam IGC. Tony Blair signed up for the Social Charter but maintained the single currency 'opt out'. The Treaty of Amsterdam led to a number of important changes. The EP was given additional powers including the right to dismiss the Commission and give its assent to international treaties including enlargement. The new treaty also incorporated 'Schengen' and introduced the concept of flexibility. Most attention centred on the measures to strengthen CFSP, especially the establishment of the position of High Representative with a supporting staff. But with the next round of enlargement unlikely to take place for at least another five years, member states were not under immediate pressure to bite the bullet of institutional reform.

The fifth enlargement 2004

The next IGC that prepared the Treaty of Nice in 2001 took place against the background of the negotiations for the fifth enlargement of the Union. This involved Estonia, Latvia, Lithuania, Poland, the Czech Republic, Hungary, Slovakia, Slovenia plus Cyprus and Malta. For the first time in the history of treaty reform substantive policy areas were absent from the Nice agenda. Instead, the IGC focused on the so-called Amsterdam leftovers, i.e. those institutional issues that should have been decided at Amsterdam.

The negotiations over the Treaty of Nice were confused, bad tempered and the result was widely regarded as a shoddy piece of work that won few friends. The member states were reluctant to contemplate a reduced size for the Commission in advance of enlargement and to accept any significant extension of QMV. Although a number of institutional changes were agreed, including a ceiling for the number of Commissioners (27) and MEPs (700), plus a complicated reform of Council votes, the changes did nothing to improve transparency in the Union (see Table 1.1). Member states seemed to recognise that the typical IGC style had run its course. There would have to be wider consultation prior to the next round of treaty reforms (Galloway 2001).

As with previous IGCs, Nice revealed divisions between Europe's leaders as to what kind of Union they desired. It also showed that the Franco-German tandem, the driving force behind previous moves for closer integration, was no longer functioning as it had in the past. In typical fashion, the disagreements at Nice were covered up by agreement to hold

Table 1.1   Weighted votes in the Council (until 2009) and seats in the European Parliament

Member state	Votes in the Council	Seats in the EP
France	29	78
Germany	29	99
Italy	29	78
United Kingdom	29	78
Poland	27	54
Spain	27	54
Netherlands	13	27
Belgium	12	24
Czech Republic	12	24
Greece	12	24
Hungary	12	24
Portugal	12	24
Austria	10	18
Sweden	10	19
Denmark	7	14
Finland	7	14
Ireland	7	13
Lithuania	7	13
Slovakia	7	14
Cyprus	4	6
Estonia	4	6
Latvia	4	9
Luxembourg	4	6
Slovenia	4	7
Malta	3	5
EU 25	321	732

yet another IGC in 2004 that would be prepared by a Convention, modelled on the body that had prepared the Charter of Fundamental Rights.

The European institutions

The European institutions will be considerably affected by enlargement from 15 to 25. Many ask how far the institutions that were created for six member states can be stretched, especially in a Union with a preponderance of small and medium-sized states. Six of the new member states will together have a population less than London, yet have more votes than the UK. Will there be perennial clashes between big and small states? A brief review of the likely impact of this enlargement on the European institutions is helpful to understand the reform agenda and to discuss the questions of legitimacy and identity.

The eurosceptic view of an all-powerful European superstate is a figment of the imagination. The EU is far from having the means or resources to form a European government. Its budget (just under 100 billion euro in 2003) is a mere 1.25 per cent of the Union's GDP, and the largest part of the budget is administered by the member states. It still spends over 80 per cent of the budget on agriculture and structural funds. Their total staff is less than 20,000, which is roughly equivalent to those employed by a small to medium-sized local authority such as Leeds or Leipzig or Lyon. These budgetary and resource limitations, agreed by member states, mean that the EU will remain almost entirely dependent on its member states and on their legislative, executive, administrative and judicial authorities for applying and controlling the rules it adopts. It is unlikely, given the different interests involved, that there will be a fundamental re-balancing in power between the member states and the institutions. What is conceivable, especially in light of enlargement, is the further development of a multi-speed Europe.

European Council

The highest authority in the Union is the European Council, comprising the heads of state and government of member states. It meets quarterly and undertakes core executive functions such as setting the agenda for the Union, resolving disputes and taking major policy decisions. Under the Convention treaty proposals, the European Council would become, for the first time, an official institution of the Union with a semi-permanent chair instead of the six-monthly rotating presidency. Several small and medium-sized states were concerned that the creation of such a position would undermine the authority of the Commission and lead to a *directoire* of the larger member states. The larger member states, however, argued that such an appointment was essential to provide for continuity and to give direction to the work of the European Council.

The Council

The Council is the body representing the ministers of member states' governments. The Council meets in various formations covering *inter alia* foreign and security policy, general affairs, economic and financial matters, justice and home affairs. The Council is the normal decision-making body reacting to proposals from the Commission that have been discussed in the EP. These ministerial meetings are prepared by an influential body of ambassadors in Brussels known as Coreper (committee of permanent representatives). Under the Convention proposals, each formation would elect its own chair for a year, except the foreign affairs council that would be chaired by the new EU foreign minister.

The Commission

The Commission has a number of tasks. It is the guardian of the treaties and responsible for overseeing the implementation of Union laws. It has a monopoly on legislative proposals, apart from CFSP and certain JHA areas. It has various executive and administrative tasks and represents the Union in areas for which it is competent. Each member state has a Commissioner who takes an oath to act independently. Until the Treaty of Nice, there were two Commissioners from the larger member states but this was changed at Nice with the larger member states gaining increased Council votes in return for giving up their second Commissioner. The new member states will each appoint a Commissioner as from 1 May 2004, the date of joining the Union, and then there will be a completely new Commission as from 1 November 2004. The main dispute concerning the Commission is whether each member state should be represented at Commissioner level. Many consider that a smaller Commission of around 15 members would ensure a more effective Commission (Cameron 2003, 'Does Size Matter', www.theepc.be). The Convention proposed a two-tier Commission in which there would be 15 full Commissioners and 15 without voting rights. It is difficult to see how such an unwieldy body could function effectively.

The European Parliament

The EP represents the democratic voice of the people. The MEPs are elected for five years under a system of proportional representation. The next elections are due in June 2004. The political parties are organised along ideological rather than national lines. The principal groups are the Socialists, the Christian Democrats, the Liberals and the Greens. The EP has steadily gained powers since the first direct elections in 1979. It now has power of co-decision over most policy areas. It is the budgetary authority and must grant assent to international agreements, including enlargement treaties.

Under the Convention proposals it would gain further powers of co-decision in areas relating to JHA and agriculture.

Two other institutions will not be greatly affected by enlargement. The Court of Justice (ECJ), based in Luxembourg, is the supreme judicial authority in the Union making judgments on cases relating to EU law. EU law supersedes national law in cases of dispute. The ECJ has one judge from each member state and is assisted by a Court of First Instance that deals with issues of lesser importance. The European Central Bank (ECB) is a relatively new institution, based in Frankfurt and oversees monetary policy for the eurozone. Each month it determines the interest rates for the eurozone. One of its main preoccupations is to fight inflation.

Democratic deficit

The EU institutions are the target for complaints about creeping centralism, the democratic deficit and lack of transparency. According to critics, power seems to flow in a one-way direction to Brussels. Where are the mechanisms for popular control? For some the answer is to increase the powers of the EP and establish a direct link between voting in EP elections and the nomination for president of the European Commission. This, it is argued, would deal with the problem of the democratic deficit and lack of transparency and reverse the decline in voting turnout for EP elections. Others argue that tackling the democratic deficit should involve a greater role for national parliaments.

The Convention was supposed to try and deal with these criticisms but apart from a modest extension of powers to the EP, it conspicuously failed to do so. The national parliaments were given a minor role to monitor subsidiarity. No powers were transferred back from Brussels to member states and the new draft treaty was no simpler to comprehend than the old treaties. This was disappointing as a number of European leaders had spoken in favour of a more radical approach. Foremost among them was Joschka Fischer, the German foreign minister, who set out his vision for the future of Europe in a famous speech at the Humboldt University in Berlin in May 2000. He argued that the enlarged EU should be organised on a federal basis with greater democracy and transparency (Fischer 2000). Fischer's speech and several high-level responses to it, notably one by French president Jacques Chirac in June 2000, led to the inclusion of a declaration in the Nice Treaty on the future of the EU. Member states called for 'a deeper and wider debate about the future development' of the EU, involving 'all interested parties: representatives of national parliaments and all those reflecting public opinion; political, economic and university circles, representatives of civil society, etc.' The debate would focus on four key questions: the delineation of competences between the EU and the member states (in keeping with the principle of subsidiarity, i.e. taking decisions at the lowest level); the status of the Charter of Fundamental

Rights; a simplification of the treaties with a view to making them clearer; and the role of national parliaments in the EU's institutional architecture. This post-Nice agenda represented the unfinished business of successive IGCs since the SEA and was to be a preparatory step for the next IGC, in 2003.

The Swedes and the Belgians, who held the presidency in 2001, were keen to promote an open debate on the future of Europe as was the European Commission that published a White Paper on Governance in the Union that summer. The Irish rejection of the Nice Treaty in a referendum in May 2001 seemed to confirm the view that there was a widening gulf between the EU and its citizens. According to most observers, the Irish were not voting against enlargement but rather expressing their disillusionment with the development of the Union. As a result the European Council agreed to establish a novel procedure to prepare the next IGC. Whereas only representatives of national governments participate in IGCs, the Council agreed that there should be representatives of national parliaments, the Commission, and the EP (and representatives from the accession states) in a Convention. Representatives from civil society were also invited to contribute their ideas.

Identity

A charge often brought by eurosceptics is the perceived loss of national identity by joining the Union. Why, argue some Estonians, should Estonia escape from the Soviet Union only to join another Union? The answer is simple. No one is forcing Estonia to join the European Union. The question of identity is not easy to resolve. Many leading British, German, Spanish and Italian soccer teams are multinational. Frenchmen manage both Arsenal and Liverpool. How does this affect identity? Turkey, Israel and Ukraine all participate in the Eurovision song contest and the European champions' league soccer competition. But many doubt that any of these countries is really 'European', or sufficiently 'European' to join the EU. Some argue that Turkey should never join the Union because it lacks a Christian identity. Christian Democrats allege that because Turkey did not participate in the enlightenment and share Europe's philosophical and religious traditions it should be excluded. Poland and the Vatican tried and failed to have a reference to Christianity inserted into the draft constitution.

Identities and loyalties change over time. In recent history people owed allegiance to city-states such as Venice and Munich before the unification of Italy and Germany. There are strong regional identities in Catalonia, Bavaria, Scotland and elsewhere in Europe. Citizens may have multiple identities to their local city, region, nation state and to Europe. What is clear is that the development of the EU has affected identities but it has not brought into question the fundamental adherence to national identities. After fifty years of the EU, the French are no less French and the Italians no less Italian.

Some of these issues were raised in the Kok report on enlargement. It noted that the EU is a very diverse, multicultural entity, destined to become even more heterogeneous as a result of enlargement, which will pose further questions of identity. With its extension to 25 and later more members, the EU will embrace widely different peoples, languages and cultures. What effect will this have on the local and national identities of its citizens? What kind of European identity is possible with such a large group of countries? How will the extended family behave? Will it be cohesive or divided? Certainly, the new members have a rich cultural heritage to share with other Europeans. In art, architecture, music, cinema, literature, their contributions to European culture is widely appreciated (Kok 2003). But these existential problems are not limited to intellectual elites. They are at the heart of some of the basic questions asked by ordinary citizens confronted by the prospect of an enlarging EU. Moreover they come at a time when mobility and migration have led to an increasingly diverse society in Europe, including immigrants from non-European countries.

Leadership in the EU

For much of the EU's history, the integration process has been driven by a strong Franco-German axis with usually beneficial results for the Union as witness the euro project. With the departure of Helmut Kohl and François Mitterrand from the scene, however, the Paris–Berlin axis has been in trouble with open disputes over the future institutional structure of the Union, the reform of the common agricultural policy (CAP) and the costs of enlargement. With the approach of the fortieth anniversary of the Franco-German Friendship (Élysée) Treaty in January 2003, Jacques Chirac and Gerhard Schroeder made a point of resolving their differences on CAP and enlargement and issued a number of joint declarations on major themes at the Convention (www.theepc.be). Both leaders understand that neither is likely to dominate the European stage alone. Chirac has often been ambivalent about the EU and has antagonised many old and new member states with his public utterances. Schroeder has never displayed much interest or enthusiasm for European integration.

The re-emergence of the Franco-German axis, however, caused some concern in other EU capitals. When Chirac and Schroeder adopted a critical position vis-à-vis the US position on the Iraq war in January 2003, other member states responded with a bout of letter diplomacy. Five member states (UK, Italy, Spain, Portugal and Denmark) plus three candidate countries (Poland, Hungary and the Czech Republic) published a letter in support of the US position. The 'gang of eight' were then supported by the 'Vilnius Ten' in another letter from central and east Europeans. This open disarray on Iraq did much damage to the Union's reputation, while strengthening ties between Paris and Berlin. The Franco-German axis will remain important in the enlarged Union but it will operate under quite different circumstances.

Self-excluded from the eurozone, Britain has sought to play a leadership role in defence issues while signalling both a more flexible approach on some sensitive issues such as increased QMV and a readiness to engage in bilateral alliances to promote national interests. The Anglo-Spanish and Anglo-Italian alliances in the approach to the Lisbon agenda and the Anglo-German proposals to make European Councils more efficient were such examples. Britain has continually called for a Europe of nation states even though Tony Blair (2000) has put forward his vision of 'Europe as a superpower, not a super state'. The UK's desire for a leadership role in the EU, however, depends on it eventually joining the euro. Given the government's decision in June 2003 to postpone a referendum on the issue, there may be a lengthy period of self-exclusion for the UK from inner circles of EU policy-making.

Italy and Spain were traditionally pro-integration countries without seeking any specific leadership role. These positions changed with the election of Silvio Berlusconi in Italy and José Maria Aznar in Spain. Both leaders have sought to form *ad hoc* alliances (often with the UK) and have not shied from playing the national card at the European table. The many allegations of corruption against Berlusconi and his propensity for political gaffes were not a conducive backdrop to Italy's tenure of the presidency in the second half of 2003. The Benelux (Belgium, Netherlands and Luxembourg) were often influential in pushing ideas in the past but in recent years political disputes in the Netherlands have reduced the Benelux voice in European affairs. The Nordic countries have also failed to make much of a mark. The Swedish 'no' in the September 2003 referendum on the euro is likely to diminish further Sweden's leadership aspirations in the EU.

As regards the institutions, in the past, the Commission often played a catalytic role in the integration process. Whether public figures, such as the first president, Walter Hallstein, or behind-the-scenes operators, such as the first secretary general, Émile Noël, the Commission has had a number of strong personalities ready to nail their colours firmly to the integrationist mast. Most observers point to the Delors era as the heyday of the Commission's role and influence (Drake 1999). To some extent this was due to the Commission's decisive role in proposing and implementing single market legislation plus its management of the PHARE programme to assist the transformation process of the former communist countries in central and eastern Europe. Perhaps more important, Delors had the backing of the two main political figures in the EU, Kohl and Mitterrand. Delors' successor, Jacques Santer, did not carry the same authority and his Commission became embroiled in disputes with the EP that led to its collective resignation in 1999. The Romano Prodi Commission (1999–2004) had to work hard to re-establish the organisation's credentials before launching new initiatives and some observers doubt whether the individual talents of its members have been harnessed successfully as a team. Furthermore, neither the EP nor its main political groupings (Christian Democrats and Social Democrats) have been able to project leadership. Outstanding parliamentarians such as Pat Cox, Gerd Poettering or Enriqe Crespo are not well known to the European public.

There are those who pin their hopes on the new proposed chair of the European Council offering leadership. Others maintain that an elected president of the Commission would be a better source of legitimacy and leadership. But the draft treaty proposals do not inspire confidence that leadership will come from anyone heading one of the institutions. Power will remain diffused between the institutions and member states. Coalitions will form on different issues. Enlargement will lead to even more promiscuous behaviour. But the leading tandem is likely to remain France and Germany even though their leadership role is unlikely ever to reach the heights it did in the 1990s.

What kind of Europe?

As the construction of Europe gradually shifts away from its initial focus, i.e. the market and the economy, towards the high politics of money, justice, foreign policy and defence, the need for 'government' is becoming more critical. Enlargement will only accelerate this trend. In the case of the single currency, the Maastricht Treaty came up with a solution: monetary policy was entrusted to an independent central bank. But solutions are still required for other policy areas. Opinion polls and most politicians agree on one point: there needs to be more Europe in foreign policy and public security. That means there needs to be more government. But what sort, and by whom? The Convention was supposed to propose a system of governance that strikes a better balance between the twin requirements of efficiency and democratic legitimacy.

Although most of the founding fathers had the vision of an eventual united states of Europe, over the years fewer and fewer politicians have advocated such a goal. The principal driving forces behind the federal Europe idea were the Christian Democrats but since the demise of Helmut Kohl there has been no political heavyweight on the centre-right in Europe willing to fight for such an objective. Indeed centre-right parties have been more concerned about the rise of extreme right-wing parties with anti-EU views. Such parties have made ground in recent years in France, Italy, Austria, Denmark, Portugal and the Netherlands, often using anti-EU rhetoric to win votes. Overall there has been a decline in ideology in the European political scene. There is now very little difference in policy terms between Labour or Social Democrats and the Christian Democrats and Liberals.

For the past decade the debate on the future of Europe has suffered from confusion over two emotive terms, federalism and sovereignty. In Britain and Scandinavia, the word federal has become associated with centralising tendencies, while in much of the rest of Europe federalism is defined as 'as much unity as necessary, as much diversity as possible'. In the US, 'federal' is simply a description of the American constitution. Although federalism implies subsidiarity (the principle that decisions are taken at the lowest possible level), the 'f word' has become so emotive that many leaders simply avoid using it. Under pressure from the UK, Giscard d'Estaing dropped the offending 'f word' from his draft treaty in June 2003.

The EU already has some attributes of a federal state and is the foremost example of sharing sovereignty in history. It has extensive powers of its own, its own budgetary resources, its own exclusive competencies and its own law, which is binding on its member states. Its four main institutions (Council, Commission, Parliament and Court) interact with each other and with the member states in a highly complex but effective manner. The complexity is due to constant negotiations, which require compromises by the member states if progress is to be made. In the final analysis, the member states are the decisive factor in the European construction and it is fanciful to suggest, as do many British eurosceptics, that they are likely to disappear in some future European government.

The EU system is thus based on a mix of supranationalism and inter-governmentalism. In the medium term it is unlikely that this mix will significantly change. Enlargement, however, will most likely bring some important changes in political culture to the Union and its institutions. The ten new member states will arrive with their own experiences in domestic and international politics. The previous western European policy process will become a pan-European policy process. It is also likely that there will be no 'one size fits all' policy-making. There are presently different regimes for CFSP, trade and the euro. Other such regimes may develop in future.

During the Convention some argued that there should be a strict division of competences, i.e. what should be done at the Union level and what should be done at the national level. A rigid approach, however, would be damaging to the EU and imply a confrontation between the EU and member states. There needs to be some flexibility to deal with changed political circumstances. For example, for many years member states opposed the Commission negotiating an air transport 'Open Skies' agreement with the US. There was a ECJ ruling in 2003, however, that paved the way for a change in competence. Similarly, there was a desire post-11 September 2001 to grant the EU more authority in JHA matters to combat terrorism.

An avant garde?

Helmut Kohl famously asked whether it was right that the slowest ship should hold up the rest of the convoy – or should those that are ready, willing and able to push ahead at a faster pace not be allowed to do so? The debate on a multi-speed Europe was sparked by the publication in

September 1994 of a Christian Democrat paper calling for a hard-core Europe. The paper argued that because of its position, its size and its close relations with France, Germany bore a special responsibility to promote an integrated wider European order. If Europe were to drift apart, Germany would once again find itself caught in the middle. Germany thus needed an integrated Europe to reassure its partners in the West and East that it had no plans to seek a *Sonderweg*. If not all member states were ready to accept further integration, then a 'hard core' should be allowed to proceed. This proposal was followed by others arguing for some form of 'variable geometry' or *à la carte* Europe. Eventually the idea of a vanguard group moving ahead of the others became enshrined in the treaties under the rubric 'enhanced cooperation'.

A multi-speed Europe already exists in several main policy areas (single currency, Schengen, defence) but although the principle of a multi-speed Europe has already been agreed, the difficulty lies in the institutional framework for such a Europe. The Convention came up with a number of proposals covering enhanced cooperation, especially in the defence field but the Commission has always rejected any idea of an organised vanguard outside the Union's structures. Prior to Amsterdam, it suggested that enhanced cooperation could proceed provided that it was compatible with the objectives of the Union, consistent with the institutional framework of the Union and open to other member states to join at any time if they were willing and able. This was largely the formula inscribed in the treaty. Since then, President Prodi has been more cautious about an avant garde. But many Brussels insiders consider that a multi-speed Europe is inevitable given the increased social and economic divergences that will result from enlargement and the political trends in the member states. From an integrationist perspective, there is certainly nothing wrong with a multi-speed Europe. Indeed, there always has been a Europe operating at different speeds. What is more worrying is a multi-vision Europe.

Conclusion

It took thirty years after the Treaty of Rome establishing the EEC in 1957 for European leaders to hold their first IGC. Since 1987, the pace has accelerated and the 2003 IGC will be the fourth in just over a decade. These IGCs have led to a substantial number of new policy areas coming within the remit of the Union but in spite of these new tasks, there remain fundamental differences between the members states on what the EU should do and how it should operate.

The main lesson to be drawn from the history of the construction of Europe is that the structure which has gradually been built up is hybrid and ambiguous. There is no more ambiguous treaty than the Treaty of Maastricht: federalist in respect of the currency, intergovernmental by virtue of its 'pillar' structure. The democratic legitimacy of the whole is itself hybrid, based in part on direct election to the Parliament and in part on the legitimacy of the governments represented in the Council. History would suggest, therefore, that the only forms of government which stand a reasonable chance of being accepted, and of managing to govern, are mixed forms, part supranational and part intergovernmental.

Given that no IGC in the past decade has been able to endow the Union with democratic legitimacy, transparency, efficiency and popular appeal, the 2003–4 IGC, which will consider the results of the Convention, faces a daunting task. It will have to agree on the powers which the EU should have to meet the internal and external challenges facing Europe, and agree also the future institutional structure for an enlarged EU with 25–30 member states. At worst it could lead to a Europe *à la carte* with weakened institutions and declining public support. At best it may provide some institutional stability for the next decade while the EU digests a dozen new members, completes the internal market and develops its role on the world stage.

References

Blair, T. (2000) 'Britain and the Future of Europe', speech in Warsaw, 6 October.

Drake, H. (2000) *Delors: Perspective of a European Leader*, London: Routledge.

Fischer, J. (2000) 'From Confederacy to Federation: Thoughts on the Finality of European Integration', speech in Berlin, 12 May.

Galloway, D. (2001) *The Treaty of Nice*, Sheffield: Sheffield Academic Press.

Kok, W. (2003) *Enlarging the European Union: Achievements and Challenges*, Florence: European University Institute.

Schonfield, A. (1974) *Journey to an Unknown Destination,* London: Royal Institute of International Affairs.

Young, H. (1999) *This Blessed Plot: Britain and Europe from Churchill to Blair*, London: Macmillan.

Further reading

Bomberg, E. and Stubb, A. (eds) (2002) *The Institutions of the European Union*, Oxford: Oxford University Press.

Corbett, R., Jacobs, F. and Shackleton, M. (1995) *The European Parliament*, London: Catermill.

Nugent, N. (2003) *The Government and Politics of the European Union*, fifth edition, London: Palgrave.

Tsoukalis, L. (2003) *What Kind of Europe?*, Oxford: Oxford University Press.

Wallace, H. and Wallace, W. (2000) *Policy-Making in the European Union*, fourth edition, Oxford: Oxford University Press.

www.europa.eu.int is the Commission portal which also leads you to other institutions and the Convention website. Much useful information can be obtained from: www.theEPC.be; www.cer.org.uk; www.eiop.or.at/erpa; www.epin.org; www.ifri.org; www.iai.it ; www.iiea.com; www.cap.uni-muenchen.de

2 The Convention and the draft constitutional treaty

David Allen

Summary

This chapter examines the Convention on the Future of Europe chaired by Valéry Giscard d'Estaing and which agreed a draft constitutional treaty for the EU in July 2003. It assesses the outcome of the Convention and the preparations for the IGC that began in October 2003 under the Italian presidency. The chapter is organised around four questions:

- Why did the Convention take place and how was it prepared?
- Who participated in the Convention and how did they work together?
- What was the output of the Convention?
- What is the likely impact of the Convention on the future of Europe?

Why did the Convention take place?

Following their failure to do so at Amsterdam (Duff 1997), the member states reached a fudged compromise at Nice on aspects of the institutional arrangements believed necessary to adapt the EU for enlargement (Galloway 2001). Even before Nice there was frustration and concern about the inadequate institutional preparations for enlargement. Accordingly, the member states at Nice initiated a process designed to consider the 'future of Europe' by which was meant the future of the enlarged European Union. The expectation was that treaty changes would be negotiated and agreed by May 2004, the target date for enlargement.

Until recently, EU treaties have been created via an IGC, which is a mechanism designed to ensure tight control of constitutional developments by the governments of the member states. IGCs themselves have sometimes been preceded by *ad hoc* meetings of either diplomats or representative politicians such as the 'Westendorp Reflection Group', which was set up in 1995 to prepare for the Amsterdam IGC. However, with the drafting of the Charter of Fundamental Rights, which was also proclaimed at Nice, a new procedure was attempted and a self-named Convention undertook the preparatory work with notable success (Deloche-Gaudez 2001). To the extent that it was an experiment, the Convention worked but this mainly because its president, Roman Herzog, was able to dominate the proceedings and drive the business forward (Ludlow 2001: 21). This method was used again in preparation for the 2003 IGC in the hope that the EU treaty-making process would be more effectively legitimised.

The Convention on the Future of Europe represents an advance on previous treaty changes but it is still flawed as a legitimising device. The Convention is meant to be deliberative and this assumes that the participants are willing and able to develop and, in some cases, change their positions. But the composition of the Convention was restricted and the procedures were to a certain extent 'rigged', whilst the use of consensus, rather than voting, to reach decisions effectively restricted the right of minorities to express their views or formally register their dissension from the views of the majority. The fact that most participants in the Convention process were anxious to establish their 'place in history' along with the Convention chairman, Valéry Giscard d'Estaing, helped the process to work but has not necessarily increased its perceived legitimacy. Europe's citizens, in some but not all the member states, will be required to endorse the ratification of the new treaty by referenda once it is agreed by the member states.

The Laeken declaration

At the end of the 2001 Belgian presidency, the European Council adopted the Laeken declaration on the Future of the European Union and announced the convening of a Convention 'in order to ensure that preparation for the forthcoming IGC is as broadly-based and as transparent as possible'. Valéry Giscard d'Estaing was appointed as chairman of the Convention with Guilliano Amato, a former Italian prime minister, and Jean-Luc Dehaene, a former Belgian prime minister, as vice-chairmen. It was agreed that all the candidate countries would take part in the Convention and that 'in parallel with the proceedings of the Convention, a Forum will make it possible to give structure to and broaden the public debate on the future of the Union that has already begun'.

The Laeken presidency conclusions also noted that, in addition to the Convention and the IGC, a number of 'additional measures' could be taken without amending the treaties. It therefore welcomed the Commission's 2001 White Paper on governance, anticipated the changes to the organisation and running of the Council that were agreed at Seville and welcomed the final report of the Madelkern high-level advisory group on the quality of regulatory arrangements.

The Laeken declaration stated that Europe was 'at a crossroads'. It identified twin challenges for the EU; the internal challenge was to bring European institutions closer to their citizens, to make them less unwieldy and more efficient and open; the external challenge was seen as the need to create a Union able to 'shoulder its responsibilities in the governance of globalisation'. The declaration related these challenges to the expectations of Europe's citizens who were perceived as calling 'for a clear, open, effective, democratically controlled Community approach, developing a Europe which points the way ahead for the world'.

The declaration posed four sets of quite detailed questions for the Convention to consider before the IGC began. These questions related to:

- the division of competences within the Union;
- the simplification of the Union's instruments;
- the need for more democracy, transparency and efficiency in the European Union – here there were a number of detailed questions about the role of the Union institutions;
- the need to reorganise the treaties, with a view to possibly adopting a 'constitutional text' for the Union including the question that had been fudged at Nice about what was to be done with the Charter of Fundamental Rights.

Finally the Laeken declaration laid out the agreed framework for the Convention establishing that it would consist of:

- the chairman and two vice-chairmen
- 15 representatives of the heads of state and government of the member states (one from each member state)
- 30 members of national parliaments (two from each member state)
- 16 members of the European Parliament
- two Commission representatives.

The accession candidate countries were represented in a similar fashion to the member states (one government representative and two national parliamentarians) and were to play a full part in the Convention except that they were not allowed to obstruct the consensus, which was the agreed method of Convention decision-making. It was also agreed that members of the Convention could be replaced by alternate members if they were not able to be present.

It was decided in advance that the Convention would appoint a directing Presidium consisting of the Convention chairman and vice-chairmen, and nine members drawn from the Convention. These nine would consist of government representatives from the three countries (Spain, Denmark and Greece) holding the Council presidency during the Convention and two representatives each from the national parliaments, the European Parliament and the Commission. Later, a representative from the accession states was added. The Presidium would also be assisted by a Convention secretariat, headed by a senior British official Sir John Kerr (a former head of the UK diplomatic service and UK permanent representative to the EU, who had been very influential in the drafting of the Maastricht Treaty).

In addition to the full Convention members and their alternates, the Economic and Social Committee, the European social partners, the Committee of the Regions and the European Ombudsman were to be invited as observers whilst the Presidents of the Court of Justice and the Court of Auditors could be invited by the Presidium to address the Convention.

The working methods of the Convention were also laid down in the Laeken declaration and it was clearly envisaged that the chairman would have a major directing role but one that could be restrained, if necessary, by the Presidium. It was agreed that the end product would be a final document, which would either reflect consensus (this was Giscard's objective from the very beginning) or record different opinions with an indication of the support that they had received. All those involved in the Convention soon realised that the latter choice would have considerably less impact on the IGC than a document that commanded consensus. In order to extend the debate beyond the Convention itself there was also to be a Forum for organisations representing civil society, a 'structured network of organisations who would receive information about the Convention's proceedings' and who would themselves input into the debate.

The Laeken declaration and the establishment of the Convention was thus yet another attempt to 're-launch' the European experiment, combined with a desperate search for ways of bringing the whole EU experience 'closer to the citizens of Europe'. Another concern revolved around the need to resolve the new division of the EU between the large and the small member states that had come to the fore at the time of the Nice negotiations. This schism, that had not impacted significantly on the development or workings of the Union before Nice, threatened the consensus on which the present and future Union depended to make progress. Whilst the debate between the 'Europeanists' and the 'Eurosceptics' is serious but heavily weighted in favour of the Europeanists in most member states, the argument between the large and the small member states was becoming more worryingly linked with the debate about the preferred future shape of the Union.

The smaller countries increasingly expressed a preference for the supranational EU institutions and procedures, in contrast to the more intergovernmentalist tendencies of the larger member states. A major task for those involved in the leadership of the Convention, therefore, was to find ways of balancing these supranational and intergovernmentalist tendencies whilst at the same time designing a Union that would be seen as legitimate by its citizens.

Who participated in the Convention and how did they work together?

The participants in the Convention came from a broader spectrum than those normally associated with IGC preparations. In addition to representatives of the governments of the member states and the candidate countries, there were also representatives from the member state and candidate countries national parliaments and the European Parliament, as well as the European Commission. Together with the chairman, Giscard d'Estaing, and his two vice-chairmen, a total of 105 'Conventioneers' (this was Giscard's preferred term as he wished to downplay the idea that they were representatives with a mandate from their respective sponsors) and, where necessary, their alternates spent a total of 52 days in plenary session as well as participating in the activities of 11 working groups. They made 1,818 interventions and spoke for over 90 hours.

They were 'observed' by representatives of the peripheral EU Committees and the social partners and their proceedings took place in public with extensive amounts (but significantly not all) of documentation and other information made publicly available on the Convention website. The secretariat received over 4,700 submissions while the website had over 700,000 'hits', with nearly 100,000 in June 2003 alone. In addition to the dissemination of information, significant efforts were also made via the Forum to involve representatives of civil society more actively. In order to participate in the Convention via the Forum, groups merely had to submit a written contribution and some 207 groups met this criterion and participated in a structured network. The Convention tried to privilege the Forum and give access to its written contributions (1,145 in all) but the one plenary session that was devoted to civil society was not a great success, probably because it was dominated by those groups who already had a formal relationship with the institutions.

Despite these efforts, which also included a youth Convention to widen participation in and access to the Convention, not that many private citizens were involved in the process and so the Convention fell well short of creating a genuine public space (Shaw 2002: 25). Eurobarometer findings support the conclusion that public knowledge and interest was not great, with the Convention remaining the least known and least trusted of all the EU institutions (even though the Convention was not an EU institution). Nevertheless the Convention does represent a significant development in the preparation of IGCs and, if the relevant provisions of the draft treaty are incorporated into the eventual constitution, it will become a permanent feature of the EU treaty-making process. It was, after all, the Convention itself that decided that its preferred outcome would be to give the Union something that was more than another treaty but which approached the idea of a constitution. The Convention began life with an open agenda and an unspecified outcome and then mandated itself to produce a draft constitutional treaty, a term that is now likely to remain when the member states conclude the IGC.

In view of the fact that the eventual outcome of the Convention (and IGC) will now certainly be regarded as a constitution for the EU, there will be those who will worry about the representation in and hence legitimacy of the Convention. The Conventioneers were predominately male; there were just 17 women full members (16 per cent) out of a total of 105 full members; only two made the 12-strong Presidium, and only one of the eleven working groups was chaired by a woman. The Convention was not particularly multicultural nor was any formal effort made to ensure the representation of minorities. Although they had personal autonomy, the Conventioneers were either nominated by the European Council or by the institutions that the European Council had selected to be represented. The member states and the EU institutions (other than the ECJ) were well represented but the regions were only indirectly represented via the observer status of six members of the Committee of the Regions. This neglect of the regions took place despite the Liège Declaration of November 2001, drawn up by the Committee of the Regions and which called for the involvement of all sub-national authorities and especially those (like Scotland) with legislative powers.

Amongst the Conventioneers it was parliamentarians who were best represented but least able to organise themselves, either because they were politically fragmented or, as was the case with many of the national parliamentarians, because they lacked institutional resources to support their activities. MEPs and MPs did, however, combine effectively towards the end of the Convention. Governmental representatives, who were pre-dominately either active or retired government ministers (10 of the 15 member states and 10 of the 13 applicant states) had excellent resource back-up as they were in effect government spokesmen. As the Convention progressed it had a tendency to become more like an IGC as several governments upped the seniority of their representatives (both France and Germany eventually sent their foreign ministers to the Convention). How-ever whilst the EU institutions (mainly the Commission and the Parliament) had few representatives they did benefit most from being based in Brussels and from having well-established links to the Convention participants. The Commission and the Parliament had four seats on the Presidium and provided the chairs for four of the 12 working groups.

The Convention accurately represented the major cleavages in European politics so that, of the 66 delegates from the current member states, 35 per cent were affiliated to the Party of European Socialist (PES), 36 per cent to the European People's Party (EPP) and 12 per cent to the European Liberal and Democratic group (ELDR). Most of the Conventioneers would probably describe themselves as pro-Europeans, although they were divided into those who advocated more or less supranationality and there was also a significant grouping of Eurosceptics, some of whom prevented a full consensus on the draft constitutional treaty being reached by issuing a minority report. Although the political parties were not formally represented in the Convention they were quite active and the EPP, the PES and the ELDR all organised meetings bringing together their supporters amongst the Conventioneers as well as submitting docu-ments to the Convention.

Undoubtedly the key role in the Convention was played by the chairman, Valéry Giscard d'Estaing, ably supported by the two vice-chairmen and Sir John Kerr, the head of the Convention secretariat. Giscard was often accused of being aristocratic and aloof but he deserves considerable credit for the fact that the Convention was able to produce a draft constitutional treaty with near complete consensus. Giscard's skill was best illustrated by the way that he successfully monopolised the reporting of the work of the Convention to both the member states and to the general public. It was usually Giscard's or Kerr's summary of proceedings that formed the ongoing basis for further negotiation. (Kerr was particularly adept at knowing the chairman's mind when he was not present and he was also both respected and feared for his ability to discover a consensus for one of Giscard's positions that not all the Conventioneers realised existed!) It was usually Giscard who created controversies (for instance his reference to the possibility of changing the name of the EU to the United States of Europe or his constant championing of the idea of a congress of the peoples of Europe) that some saw as clever diversions or as negotiating positions that were designed to be conceded in return for consensus on more important items. Many Conventioneers complained that Giscard in effect hijacked the Convention but then many of them willingly went along with this because of their shared desire to book their place in history as one of the founders of the new European constitution. Probably Giscard deserves most credit for his decision to postpone the discussion of the institutional framework until the very end of the Convention. Giscard's view was that it would be easier to reach agreement on this, the most contentious of issues, once the Convention had already heavily invested in agreement on all the other issues. He justified this quite reasonably by arguing that the task should define the institutions and not vice versa.

Nevertheless, Giscard and Kerr did not have it all their own way, nor did they always agree with each other. The Presidium, which was established and selected by the European Council, provided the input for the Convention to work with; it drafted the agenda, it structured the contacts with civil society and it managed the activities of the various working groups. There were clearly tensions within the Presidium, which was by no means a coherent team. At times the wider grouping felt it necessary to challenge the chairman and in so doing it was assisted by the willingness of one or both of the vice-chairmen to lead the revolt. This happened most publicly towards the end of the Convention when Giscard published a version of the institutional proposals that was then dramatically revised by the Presidium.

Despite the tensions, the Presidium and the chairman were united in their desire to try and achieve consensus. The working method usually revolved around an initial debate on a paper presented by the Presidium, often incorporating material from the working groups, with regular updating summaries being issued. The views of the Conventioneers, both oral and written, were thus regularly 'summarised' by the secretariat and the Presidium and returned to the Convention in the shape of new papers. Votes were never taken and so the existence of a consensus on any particular issue (or on the draft constitutional treaty as whole) was essentiality determined by the chairman and the Presidium.

The Presidium made use of 11 working groups (six were established in May 2002, four more in September 2002 and a final one in November 2002). Membership of these working groups was open and Conventioneers were not limited (other than by their own interest, expertise and availability) to any one group. The Presidium kept firm control over the working groups in order to avoid dividing the Convention. The working groups were constrained as to time, had restricted agendas and were required to examine specific issues and questions that arose from the plenary sessions.

In all these activities the applicant states played their part, although for many of the representatives, especially those from the national parliaments, there was a very steep learning curve. Although the applicants participated on the basis of equal representation they did not formally make up the consensus behind the draft constitutional treaty or rather they were not allowed to act in such a way as to prevent a consensus being established. This was regarded as fair because it was not clear at the beginning of 2002 that all the applicant states would be ready to join in the next two years.

Although there was much speculation about the ability of the Convention to deliver an outcome capable of significantly impacting on the forthcoming IGC it did prove possible. In the eighteen months of its existence the Convention managed to firmly establish the idea that its output should and could be a draft constitutional treaty and that the chances of such a document setting the agenda for the eventual treaty would be high if consensus on its content could be achieved. There were those who were disappointed with the draft treaty described below but the achievement of the Convention in producing it with so few dissenters is a considerable one in the circumstances.

What was the outcome of the Convention?

After much last-minute negotiation and with one or two issues still to be finally resolved, Valéry Giscard d'Estaing presented a draft constitutional treaty to the European Council at its meeting in Thessalonica on 19–20 June 2003. The presidency conclusions noted that this thus marked the completion of the Convention's tasks, as set out at Laeken, although the definitive version of the draft treaty was eventually completed only on 15 July with the final drafting of Part Three. The Council saw the draft constitutional treaty as a 'good basis for starting the IGC' and requested the Italian presidency to convene the IGC in October 2003 with a view to completing the constitutional treaty 'as soon as possible'. The deadline for completion was to be set so as to allow the treaty to 'become known to

European citizens' before the June 2004 elections for the European Parliament. It was agreed that the acceding states would participate fully in the IGC on an equal basis and that the treaty would be signed by the member states of the enlarged Union 'as soon as possible after 1 May 2004'. It was also agreed that the three candidate countries, Bulgaria, Romania and Turkey, would participate in the IGC as observers.

The draft constitution would create a Union with a single legal personality founded upon a single treaty (there is provision for the repeal of all the previous treaties from the date of entry into force of the treaty establishing the constitution). There is a rather long and wordy Preamble followed by four substantive Parts. Part One describes the Union's 'Constitutional Structure' and is divided into ten Titles and 59 Articles, which together lay out the general principles determining the Union's values, objectives, competences, institutions, procedures, instruments and finances.

Part Two brings the Charter of Fundamental Rights into the draft treaty and is divided into seven Titles and 54 Articles. Part Three has seven Titles, some of which are divided again into Chapters, Sections and Sub-Sections, and deals in greater detail with the 'Policies and Functioning of the Union'. Part Four covers the General and Final Provisions and is divided into nine Articles.

The substance of the draft treaty is a clever compromise, masterminded by Giscard d'Estaing, and designed to appeal to both the 'federalists' and the 'intergovernmentalists'. The draft treaty contains some major changes to the EU's institutional and procedural arrangements and some more modest changes to the EU's competences. Unlike the SEA and the TEU, the draft treaty does not contain a spectacular new objective such as the single market or Economic and Monetary Union. What it does contain is a better attempt than previous treaties at reforming the workings of the EU to meet the challenge of enlargement. It is not possible to do full justice to all the proposals that can be found in the draft treaty and, in any case, some may well be modified by the member states when they meet in the IGC. However, it seems unlikely that the IGC will attempt to change too much of the basic structure of the treaty. The central involvement of the member state governments in the Convention process and the determination of Giscard in particular to deliver a treaty that he thought they could live with has probably ensured that most of what has been proposed will remain. When presenting the draft treaty to the European Council in June 2003, Giscard was careful to point out that it constituted a 'coherent and unequivocal whole' and that it represented 'the best balance' between the role of the Union and that of the member states. The clear implication was that the whole and the balance should not be interfered with.

Giscard sees the draft treaty as successfully responding to two major requests from the European Council:

1 for the European system to be clarified and simplified,
2 for the creation of new tools to develop further all aspects of the Union which he took to mean the traditional Community policy areas plus CFSP and JHA.

The draft looks to meet the first of these issues in a number of ways:

- by clarifying the allocation of competences between the Union and the member states. The draft distinguishes between 'exclusive competences' of the Union, 'shared competences' between the Union and the member states and 'areas of supporting action'. The idea here is to reassure those states who fear creeping integration; the Union's competencies will be agreed and fixed and only changed by a revision of the constitution.
- by creating a mechanism to control the application of the principle of subsidiarity by allowing for the direct involvement of national parliaments in the EU legislative process. Legislative proposals will be sent to national parliaments as well as to the EP and the Council. National parliaments will have two votes each (to allow for single and double chamber parliaments) and, if one-third of the total votes call for it, the Commission will be obliged to reconsider (or even withdraw) its proposal in light of the subsidiarity principle. This may please the national parliaments but it also threatens to bring domestic politics into the EU legislative process.
- by simplifying the Union's legal instruments. The draft reduces the number of such instruments from 15 to 6 – legislative acts will either be 'European laws' (old-style regulations) or 'European framework laws' (old-style directives). The procedure for making legislative acts has also been simplified in that the interim cooperation procedure finally disappears and the co-decision procedure is renamed as the ordinary legislative procedure. Whilst there will continue to be important exceptions, the draft treaty increases the areas in which co-decision is used from 37 to around 80 and this is certainly a significant evolution of the EU's legislative procedures. Again, whilst there will continue to be exceptions vital to the interests of individual member states, the assumption is that co-decision will also normally involve the use of QMV in the Council. The draft also establishes a hierarchy of legal norms headed by legislative acts followed by non-legislative acts ('European regulations' (implementing acts) and 'European decisions' followed by 'non-binding acts' (recommendations and opinions). There is also a new category of 'delegated regulation'.
- by conferring a single legal personality on the Union, which means that the European Union will be able to sign treaties. This also means that all the previous treaties will be repealed when the constitutional treaty is agreed and ratified.

- by abolishing the pillar structure established by the TEU and replacing it with a simpler single structure. However, the spirit of the pillar structure remains in Part Three of the treaty, which retains separate procedures for the CFSP/ESDP and certain aspects of JHA.

In seeking to meet the demand for 'more Europe' the draft treaty proposes:

- to fully develop an area of freedom, security and justice in response to a strong public demand. With the removal of the third pillar, this will involve the application of a common legal framework including the extension of QMV to most policy areas. This represents a major integrative advance and brings the area of justice and home affairs fully into the Union legal system. Giscard (2003) saw these developments as significant in relation to European citizens, arguing that from their point of view Europe 'will have two of the features on which the communal life of people is based: a currency and justice'.
- to fully integrate the external policy of the Union by creating the post of EU minister for foreign affairs, a merging of the jobs currently held by Javier Solana as the EU's High Representative for CFSP and by Chris Patten as the Commissioner for External Relations. The proposal is that the foreign minister will be appointed by and answerable to the European Council, chair the Foreign Affairs Council and also be a Vice-President of the Commission so that s/he can 'ensure coordination between all aspects of EU external policy'. This is a major change, which was initially opposed by both Solana and Patten. It is an enormous portfolio and there will clearly be problems for the individual concerned in trying to maintain a position in both the Commission and the Council. The treaty also contains proposals to establish a single bureaucratic structure to support the European foreign minister, bringing together officials from the Commission, the Council Secretariat and the national diplomatic services. It would create an European external action service out of the present Commission external delegations.
- to further develop ESDP by extending the Petersberg tasks to include joint disarmament operations, military advice and post-conflict stabilisation and by establishing a European armaments, research and military capabilities agency. The draft treaty also provides for some member states to work more closely together in 'structured cooperation' and there is a mutual solidarity clause in case of either terrorism or natural disaster. In addition, there is a mutual defence clause, which is open to all who might wish to adhere to it, similar to that found in the old WEU Treaty and in Article V of NATO.
- to further develop the economic governance of the Union by improving coordination procedures between the member states. Here there is an attempt to strengthen the role of the Commission in highlighting

divergences between the member states' economic policies as well as their budgetary deficits. Despite the objections of those states which are not yet members of the eurozone, the treaty goes some way towards further recognition of the specificity of those using the euro, allowing a two and a half year presidency for the Eurozone Council and recognising the need for these countries to take certain decisions apart from the Economic and Finance Council.

Finally and most significantly, the draft treaty makes a number of proposed changes to the institutions and procedures of the Union. It is these proposals that are probably most vulnerable to modification by the member states in the IGC, even though they represent an obvious attempt by Giscard to balance the interests of federalist and intergovernmentalists and large and small member states.

The draft recognises the dual nature of the EU (a Union of peoples and of states) in which the 'member states confer competences on the Union to attain objectives that they have in common' (Article 1). For its part the Union operates through an 'institutional triangle' of the European Parliament, the European Commission and Council, all of which have to be kept in balance if the system is to be acceptable to all concerned.

According to Giscard (2003) the European Parliament is the 'big winner' under the draft treaty because of the establishment of co-decision as the ordinary legislative procedure and its extension to many new areas of Union activity. However, given the additional authority that is planned for the European Council, it is hard to substantiate this claim even though the budgetary powers of the EP are also confirmed and extended for the first time to include a proper say in agricultural expenditure. The draft treaty also has something to say about the composition of the EP after 2009 (in the 2004–9 period that the numbers agreed at Nice will apply). The proposal is that the composition of the Parliament will be established, as before, according to a degressively proportional rule with a minimum of four seats for the smallest member state. A complication arises because of the delayed entry of Bulgaria and Romania. As they will not have joined the Union by the 2004 elections the seats they were allocated at Nice will be redistributed to the other member states up to the Nice ceiling of 732 seats. When Romania and Bulgaria do eventually join they will have 33 and 17 seats respectively but the European Council will have to agree a further redistribution in time for the 2009 elections in order to keep within the target of 732 seats.

Giscard failed in his repeated attempts to get the Convention to accept a Congress that would bring national and European parliamentarians together but when he presented the draft treaty to the European Council he made a point of referring to it again, claiming that if a 'European political authority' is to emerge one day, it will demand greater cooperation between national and European parliamentarians.

A better candidate for the 'big winner' prize would seem to be the European Council, which becomes a full European institution mandated to provide the dynamics to drive the Union forward and to define its general political direction and priorities. Previously the European Council, like the other manifestations of the Council, had been managed by the rotating presidency but the larger states in particular have expressed a growing frustration with this organising device. The draft treaty provides for an elected (by the other members of the European Council) president who would serve for a two and a half year term with the opportunity for a maximum of two terms. The new president is given the same tasks as those carried out by the six monthly rotating presidency: chairing the European Council, working with the president of the Commission and the General Affairs Council to prepare the work of the European Council, working to ensure cohesion and consensus within the Council and ensuring 'at his level' the external representation of the Union on issues concerning the CFSP. Interestingly the proviso is added that this latter task must be undertaken 'without prejudice to the responsibilities of the new foreign minister'. The Council president is not due to be elected in this manner until the treaty enters into force (possibly 2006) so if the foreign minister is appointed at an earlier date, as seems likely, s/he will have a head start as far as external representation is concerned. Nevertheless, one still fears that the European Council president and the EU foreign minister (not to mention the president of the Commission) will continue to lead outside observers to speculate about 'who speaks for Europe'.

Despite the new arrangements for electing the president of the Council, the rotating presidency has not been entirely eliminated. A yearly rotation is retained for the sectoral Councils. The draft treaty proposes that the Council should be refocused around two major configurations; Foreign Affairs and the General and Legislative Affairs Council. The idea of a Legislative Council is designed to separate out the legislative and executive roles of the Council and to enable the legislative role to become more transparent. The Foreign Affairs Council will be chaired by the foreign minister but the General Affairs and Legislative Council, as well as the additional Council formations that will be decided upon by the European Council, will be chaired by a variant of the rotating presidency. These Councils will be chaired by the member states on the basis of 'equal rotation for periods of at least one year'.

The draft treaty makes a significant and simplifying change to the system of QMV. Like co-decision, QMV becomes the default system of voting in the Council but, not surprisingly, exceptions remain of which the most significant is the continued use of unanimity for CFSP/ESDP decision-making, something that is hard to reconcile with an enlarged Council of 25 members. The draft treaty establishes that a qualified majority will consist of a simple majority of member states representing three-fifths (60 per cent) of the population of the Union. This is a significant departure from the complicated voting weights agreed at Nice and a number of member states led by Spain and Poland remain deeply unhappy at what they see as their relative loss of influence under the new arrangements. This system is due to be introduced in November 2009 after the European elections and after the new Commission has been appointed. Although the draft treaty allows for a number of exceptions to the general rule that QMV shall prevail (taxation, immigration quotas for labour markets and the cultural aspects of trade will all continue to require unanimity to satisfy the particular interests of the UK, Germany and France), it also provides a means whereby the European Council can decide unanimously to apply QMV to any area of policy without requiring the ratification of a treaty change. This so-called 'bridging clause' will be the subject of some member state opposition even though they remain protected by the initial unanimity requirement.

The European Commission probably has least reason to be satisfied with the orientation of the draft treaty, although the Commission is as aware as Giscard was of the necessity of coming up with a set of institutional arrangements satisfactory to the member states. Some would have liked the Commission to have its own president directly elected but this was never likely. The emphasis in the draft treaty is on a return to the original concept of the Commission as a high-level body responsible mainly for defining and proposing the common European interest (as opposed to the individual national interests advanced by the member states) and for facilitating member state agreement as to Union objectives and instruments. The Commission retains its exclusive right of initiative with regard to legislative acts and its role in the area of justice and home affairs has also been expanded.

The composition of the Commission is part of a general wrangle between the larger and smaller states, with the larger states anxious to restrict membership of the College in the interests of efficiency. The smaller member states, concerned that their larger brethren will increase their dominance of the Union, are keen not to lose their entitlement to a Commissioner. The result is yet another compromise, with the draft treaty providing from 2009 onwards for a College with a maximum of 15 full members, including the president and the foreign minister. Giscard (2003) rather slyly referred to the fact that he thought that it would be good for the member states of the enlarged Union to experience between 2004 and 2009 the 'problems of ensuring that a College of 25 members functions efficiently'. The compromise comes in the form of a suggestion that the Commission be 'supplemented by the appointment of non-voting Commissioners from all the member states that are not included in the College'. The treaty provides for an equal rotation of full Commissioners and non-voting Commissioners and so the principle of *juste retour* will be preserved at the expense of the principle of appointing Commissioners solely on merit. Once the Commission president is nominated by the European Council and formally 'elected' by the EP, he will get to select his Commission from lists of three potential candidates (the list must include candidates of both genders) put forward by the member states.

Most observers consider that the institutional proposals in the draft treaty are not that radical but they are realistic. The history of the Union suggests that political will rather than the precise nature of the institutional arrangements will be what determines the success or not of the proposals being included in the final treaty. Provided the political will exists to make the institutions work, these arrangements should prove workable for some time. It remains to be seen whether the enlarged Union can generate that political will.

What will be the impact of the Convention?

The immediate impact of the Convention's work was positive, with most member states broadly welcoming the draft treaty. Of course most member states had something that they wished to change and the last month of the Convention saw some hectic bargaining over the specific details that were included in Part Three of the draft treaty. The European Council agreed to give the Convention three more weeks to conclude what were described as 'technical details' but by then the member states were not in the mood for serious revision of the draft, preferring instead to wait for the IGC to begin in the autumn.

It is unlikely that the IGC will seek to unravel the broad agreement that Giscard and his fellow Conventioneers have managed to put together although there will undoubtedly be continuing arguments about some of the particulars. Most observers seem to agree that the Preamble could be more economically worded and few seem impressed by the worst compromise of them all, the decision to appoint non-voting Commissioners in order to maintain the principle of equal member state representation on the Commission. On the other hand the British seem content with the arrangements for including the Charter of Fundamental Rights in Part Two of the treaty whilst making it clear that it only applies to matters related to Union policies and competences and not more generally to all aspects of life within the member states.

There is some concern about the fluidity of the situation between the beginning of the IGC and 2009. The new members will play a full part in the IGC to decide the new treaty but as they join in 2004 a number of significant changes will occur before the new treaty is ratified, provided it is agreed unanimously. In 2004 there will be direct elections to the European Parliament followed by the selection (and confirmation) of the new Commission president as well as the new 25-member Commission. At the end of 2004 Mr Solana's mandate will expire as will that of Commissioner Patten. It remains to be seen whether the new EU foreign minister, with one foot in the Council and one in the Commission, will be appointed before the new treaty is ratified or indeed if the Convention's proposal survives the IGC. If the new treaty is agreed in 2004, the question of ratification will arise and there must be some doubt as to whether all 25 member states will be able to ratify what is likely to be perceived as a far-reaching and controversial treaty. It is already clear that many of the EU member states will either wish to or will feel obliged to put any new treaty to their citizens in the form of a referendum. There is, for example, strong pressure in the UK for a dual referendum on the new treaty and the euro. Even if the new treaty is agreed and ratified by the end of 2006, there will probably be some momentum for further revision from those, not fully satisfied with the initial deal. Further revision may prove difficult if the member states are, by 2006, locked into predictable wrangles about the next budgetary perspective (budgetary perspectives are recognised in the draft treaty as 'the multi-annual financial framework').

The draft treaty has avoided dealing with the situation that might arise if one or more member states have problems ratifying the new treaty. The draft passes the buck to the European Council. Article V 7 of Part Four simply states that 'if, two years after the signature of the treaty establishing the constitution, four-fifths of the member states have ratified it and one or more member states have encountered difficulties in proceeding with ratification, the matter shall be referred to the European Council'. It would be presumably up to the European Council to then decide whether a member state that could not ratify the constitution should be asked to accept a second-class membership or to leave the Union.

Conclusion

The Convention has almost certainly established itself as an essential part of any future treaty revision process. Giscard and his fellow Conventioneers would probably like to think that they have established the essential foundations on which the future Union can now be built. It remains to be seen whether Giscard's claim that his draft treaty could last 'for fifty years' is valid but it is probably already the case that unravelling it would be a backward step that the Union could ill afford.

References

Deloche-Gaudez, F. (2001) *The Convention on a Charter of Fundamental Rights: A Method for the Future?* Paris: Notre Europe, Research and Policy Paper No. 15.

Duff, A. (ed) (1997) *The Treaty of Amsterdam: Text and Commentary*, London: Federal Trust, Sweet and Maxwell.

European Commission (2001) *White Paper on Governance*, COM (2001) 428 final 25.7.01.

Galloway, D. (2001) *The Treaty of Nice and Beyond*, Sheffield: Sheffield Academic Press.

Giscard d'Estaing, V. (2003) 'Oral report presented to the European Council in Thessalonica', Brussels: The European Convention, SN/173/03.

Ludlow, P. (2001) *A View from Brussels: A Commentary on the EU: 2004 and Beyond*, Brussels: Centre for European Policy Studies.

Shaw, J. (2002) *Process, Responsibility and Inclusion in EU Constitutionalism: The Challenge for the Convention on the Future of Europe*, London: Federal Trust.

Further reading

Clegg, N. (2003) 'Europe deserves a respite from this upheaval', *Financial Times*, 9 July.

Committee of the Regions (2001) Liège Declaration (http://europa.eu.int/futurum/conoth_en.htm#po).

Economist (2003) Special Report on Europe's Constitution, 21 June.

European Council (2003) *Presidency Conclusions, Thessalonica European Council, 19–20 June* (http://ue.eu.int/en/Info/eurocouncil/index.htm).

European Council (2001) *Presidency Conclusions, Laeken European Council, 14–15 December* (http://ue.eu.int/en/Info/eurocouncil/index.htm).

European Policy Centre (2003) 'The draft constitutional treaty – an assessment', EPC Issue Paper no. 5, 3/7/2003.

Everts, S. and Keohane, D. (2003) 'An unconventional bargain', *Centre for European Reform Bulletin*, Issue 30, June/July.

Federal Trust (2003) 'The Convention during its final weeks', *The EU Constitution Project Newsletter*, Volume 1, Issue 4, July, pp. 2–4 (www.fedtrust.co.uk/EU_constitution).

Grabbe, H. (2003) *The CER Guide to the Draft European Constitution*, London: Centre for European Reform.

Hoffman, L. and Verges-Bausili, A. (2003) 'The reform of Treaty revision procedures: The Convention on the Future of Europe', in Bozel, T. and Cichowski, R. (eds) *The State of the European Union VI: Law, Politics and Society*, Oxford: Oxford University Press

Parker, G. and Dombey, D. (2003) 'Not perfect but more than we could have hoped for', *Financial Times*, 20 June, p. 19.

Philippart, E. (2002) 'The European Convention: Anatomy of the new approach to constitution-making in the EU', *European Union Studies Association* (EUSA) *Review*, Vol. 15, No. 2, pp. 5–7.

Weiler, J.H.H. (2002) 'A Constitution for Europe? Some hard choices', United Kingdom: *Journal of Common Market Studies*, Vol. 40, No. 4, pp. 563–80.

3 The enlargement negotiations

Graham Avery

Summary

This chapter concerns the enlargement negotiations that took place from 1998 to 2003, leading to the accession of ten countries to the European Union in 2004. It describes the conduct of the negotiations, their main stages, and the principal problems encountered, but it also places them in the wider context of the applicant countries' preparation for membership, and of the overall accession process that will continue.

Background

After the historic events of the late 1980s and early 1990s, the fall of the Berlin Wall, the collapse of communism, and the end of Soviet domination, one of the first decisions of the countries of central and eastern Europe was to turn to the West for admission to the 'Euro-Atlantic' framework, in particular through membership of the EU and NATO.

The EU was swift to offer financial assistance in 1989 through the PHARE programme, subsequently extended to all the states of central and eastern Europe, and to sign 'association' agreements (also known as 'Europe' agreements) with them from 1991 onwards. Although these accords provided for cooperation in political, economic, cultural and other areas – including a large degree of liberalisation of trade in non-agricultural goods – and for adoption of important parts of EU rules and policies, they fell significantly short of the countries' aspiration for EU membership. The preamble of the agreements recognised membership as the wish of the associated states, without affirming it as the aim of the EU.

The reunification of Germany in 1990 effectively 'enlarged' the EU through the integration of the German Democratic Republic into its Western neighbour. The other former communist countries were determined to join the EU too, not only for symbolic reasons – as a return to the European family from which they had been separated in the aftermath of the war – but for basic political and economic reasons. In terms of security, they perceived EU membership as a supplement to NATO membership because of the powerful 'bonding' effect of its institutions and policies, and it would also bring economic gains through full access to the EU's market and budgetary receipts from its policies.

Copenhagen: the promise of membership

Hesitations on the EU side concerning eastern enlargement persisted in the early 1990s, with attention focused on other political priorities such as the creation of the single market, the negotiation of the Maastricht Treaty, and the preparation for the EFTA enlargement which brought Austria, Sweden and Finland into the EU in 1994.

But in June 1993 a historic step was taken at the European Council in Copenhagen, when the EU's leaders stated that 'the associated countries of central and eastern Europe that so desire shall become members of the Union. Accession will take place as soon as a country is able to assume the obligations of membership by satisfying the economic and social conditions.'

This was the first time that the EU promised membership to any countries, even before they applied for it, and the promise was accompanied, for the first time, by a statement of the conditions for membership. The 'Copenhagen criteria' stated that membership of the Union requires that a country

> has achieved stability of institutions guaranteeing democracy, the rule of law, human rights and respect for and protection of minorities; the existence of a functioning market economy, as well as the capacity to cope with competitive pressure and market forces within the Union; the ability to take on the obligations of membership, including adherence to the aims of political, economic and monetary union.

This group of three types of criterion, political, economic and administrative (the ability to take on the obligations of membership), was accompanied by a fourth criterion linking enlargement to the EU's internal reform, since 'the Union's capacity to absorb new members, while maintaining the momentum of European integration, is also an important consideration'.

In 1994 the first applications for membership were presented by Hungary and Poland, followed in 1995 and 1996 by eight applications from other countries of central and eastern Europe. In July 1997 the European Commission produced a detailed report on enlargement, with its ten Opinions on the applicant (or 'candidate') countries and its 'Agenda 2000' proposals for the development of the EU's policies and budget for the period 2000–6.

Taking account of their progress in fulfilling the Copenhagen criteria, the Commission recommended opening accession negotiations with five countries of central and eastern Europe (Hungary, Poland, Estonia, Czech Republic, Slovenia) plus Cyprus. For the others, it concluded that the political criterion was not yet fulfilled by Slovakia, and the economic and administrative criteria were not sufficiently fulfilled by Latvia, Lithuania, Romania and Bulgaria. The decision of the European Council at Luxembourg in December 1997 to open negotiations with the first six countries led to their designation as the 'Luxembourg group' and when in December 1999 the European Council at Helsinki decided to extend them to six more countries, they became known as the 'Helsinki group'. A detailed chronology of the stages of the enlargement process is given in Table 3.1

The preparation for membership

From the outset, the strategy of the EU was to link accession and the accession negotiations to the preparation of the applicant countries for membership, making their progress to membership conditional on adequate preparation 'on the ground'. The Commission stated in 1997 'the actual timetable for accession will depend primarily on the progress made by individual countries in adopting, implementing and enforcing the *acquis*'. It wished them to take on as much as possible of the *acquis* before membership, though it accepted that transitional periods might be necessary. Emphasising that membership conferred rights as well as obligations, it said that 'the new member states should accept the basic obligations on accession, otherwise their right to participate fully in the decision-making process may be put into question' and in particular it insisted that 'the measures necessary for the single market should be applied immediately'.

Table 3.1 Chronology of the enlargement process

	Application	Opinion of Commission	Start of negotiations	End of negotiations	Accession
Turkey	14.4.87	14.12.89			
Cyprus	4.7.90	30.6.93	31.3.98	5.2.03	1.5.04
Malta	16.7.90	30.6.93	15.2.00	5.2.03	1.5.04
Hungary	31.3.94	16.7.97	31.3.98	5.2.03	1.5.04
Poland	5.4.94	16.7.97	31.3.98	5.2.03	1.5.04
Romania	22.6.95	16.7.97	15.2.00		
Slovakia	27.6.95	16.7.97	15.2.00	5.2.03	1.5.04
Latvia	13.10.95	16.7.97	15.2.00	5.2.03	1.5.04
Estonia	24.11.95	16.7.97	31.3.98	5.2.03	1.5.04
Lithuania	8.12.95	16.7.97	15.2.00	5.2.03	1.5.04
Bulgaria	14.12.95	16.7.97	15.2.00		
Czech Republic	17.1.96	16.7.97	31.3.98	5.2.03	1.5.04
Slovenia	10.6.96	16.7.97	31.3.98	5.2.03	1.5.04
Croatia	21.2.03				

Notes:
The countries mentioned are those whose applications were active in mid-2003. For the chronology of preceding applications see G. Avery and F. Cameron 1998: 25–6.
'End of negotiations' is date of final agreement on text of Treaty of Accession.

The EU therefore reinforced the 'pre-accession strategy' for the countries of central and eastern Europe with increased financial aid, accession partnerships linking financial assistance to priorities concerning the political and economic criteria and the adoption of the *acquis* and regular reports by the Commission on their progress. For the applicant countries, these were onerous conditions, which sometimes they felt were designed to delay rather than facilitate enlargement, particularly since the EU resisted their appeals for a 'target' date to be set for accession. Even after the promise at Copenhagen, there seemed to be a fear of eastern enlargement on the part of some member states.

Nevertheless, the EU's enlargement strategy had a remarkable success. Because of the conditionality of the accession process, linking the timetable for membership to the fulfilment of the criteria and its 'transparency' through the publication of reports each year, it was possible for the applicant countries to accelerate their reforms in the decade that followed the promise in Copenhagen. Stable democracies emerged, with well-functioning democratic institutions and increased respect for minorities. The economic transition from central planning was completed with an inflow of investment and growth rates higher than the EU average. Although the process was encouraged by financial assistance not only from the EU but also from other international institutions, it is clear that the prospect of accession, the 'golden carrot', played a key role in encouraging reforms. The resulting stability and increasing prosperity has been of benefit to western Europeans: for example, trade between the ten central and east European countries and the EU doubled in the period 1995–2000.

Moreover, the preparation for membership by the applicant countries in fields other than economic policy has also been of benefit to citizens in the EU. For example, in the fight against crime and terrorism these countries have increased police and judicial cooperation in the enforcement of laws, so that international traffic in drugs and humans is easier to control. The protection of their frontiers with non-EU countries is improving and they are cooperating to regulate the flow of immigrants and asylum-seekers from elsewhere. In the environmental field the application of EU rules on pollution of air and water is making their environment safer for their own citizens and for neighbouring countries and they are encouraged to con-serve their rich bio-diversity and natural heritage of species and habitats. The EU has insisted on bringing their nuclear power plants up to higher levels of safety.

Conduct of the negotiations

The accession negotiations began on 31 March 1998 with a series of separate meetings with the six countries at ministerial level. For the EU the president of the Council made a statement (identical for all countries) on the procedures and principles of the negotiations, to which the applicants replied, indicating in some cases the important questions for them in the negotiations.

The procedure for these negotiations was identical with that for previous accession negotiations (Avery and Cameron 1998): conferences of an intergovernmental character held separately between the EU and each of the applicants, with regular meetings at the level of ministers (normally foreign ministers) or their deputies (with the rank of ambassadors: for the applicant countries their chief negotiators, and for the EU members their permanent representatives in Brussels). The 'bilateral' nature of the process, with individual accession conferences, was an important structural factor of the negotiations: on the one hand it rendered it difficult for the applicant countries to present a common front to the EU, but on the other hand it maintained the principle that each country was treated separately on its own merits (the principle of 'differentiation').

It is sometimes argued that the bilateral structure of the negotiations was inspired by a 'divide-and-rule' strategy on the part of the EU. But the applicants were just as insistent as the EU on the principle of differentiation in the negotiations, since they did not wish the progress of their accession to be linked to that of others. For the EU the application of differentiation was simple enough in theory, but not so easy in practice, since any 'concession' to one applicant was likely to be claimed by the others in their negotiations. Thus, although the Commission prepared individual positions for the EU to present to each country, they were often similar or even identical, because of the need for a coherent overall approach.

Despite the fact that the applicant countries held meetings together, particularly the six members of the 'Luxembourg group', who regularly met at the level of ministers or chief negotiators, and the Višegrad group of Hungary, Poland, Slovakia and the Czech Republic, there was little real coordination of positions; for the budgetary questions, particularly agriculture, where all the applicant countries strongly opposed the EU's position, there was a more vigorous effort to present a common line, but it had little impact on the final result.

The organisation of the negotiations on the EU side was the same as in previous accession negotiations: EU positions and statements were delivered to the applicant countries by the country holding the presidency of the Council, acting as the EU's spokesman. The role of the Commission in the formal sessions of the accession conferences was secondary, although it was regularly asked to explain or defend the EU's point of view. Outside, however, the Commission played a pivotal role in the negotiations, not only through its right of initiative but also because of the highly technical nature of many of the matters under discussion. For the applicant countries, moreover, the Commission was perceived as an 'honest broker', seeking to find solutions in the interest of the enlarged EU rather than of the existing member states.

The 'common positions', which the presidency presented to the applicants, normally in writing before the sessions of the conference, were proposed by the Commission as 'draft common positions' and then approved by the Council by unanimous consent. They were not sent to the European Parliament (another intergovernmental aspect of the procedure) and in fact were considered to be confidential documents, not accessible to the public. But in practice they rapidly passed into the hands of the Brussels press corps and were reported widely, with the result that there was often a lively public debate on such proposals before they were approved by the Council.

Because of the procedure for adoption of positions by the EU, involving discussion of proposals in the Council's Enlargement Group (a sub-committee bringing together diplomatic and expert representatives of the member states) and approval by the Committee of Permanent Representatives or the Council itself at ministerial level (foreign ministers), the time taken by the EU to reach its positions was in some cases longer than that available for the applicant countries to respond. But in reality the negotiating process began long before the stage of the Commission's proposals: these were normally preceded by exploratory contacts with the countries concerned, which continued during the discussions on the EU side, when the applicant countries often signalled publicly, or privately, their reactions.

The sessions of the accession conferences were usually brief and scripted in advance, a kind of 'liturgy' in which each side generally delivered formal speeches, not providing the chance for real discussion or negotiation in the proper sense. This was a source of irritation to the applicant countries in the earlier stages of the negotiations, particularly when the EU's positions lacked substance, or they could obtain no reply to questions or requests. Given the fact that the EU's positions had to be agreed by unanimity, the presidency had little flexibility to respond immediately. The real negotiations took place between meetings and the applicant countries soon realised that the road to agreement lay not only through Brussels but also through the capitals of member states.

The *acquis*

A key feature of accession negotiations is the principle that applicant countries have to accept, without modification, the EU's *acquis* – its accumulated rules and policies. Thus the scope of the negotiations is limited to the possibility of delays in applying the rules during 'transitional periods'.

For the negotiations which commenced in 1998 the *acquis* was divided into 31 chapters (Table 3.2). This articulation of the EU's rules into chapters is specific to accession negotiations (they are classified in different ways in other EU contexts) and it follows a logical sequence in which the policies related to the single market come first, followed by other internal policies, then external affairs and finally – to mark their importance and the fact that they are traditionally handled at the end of negotiations – the chapters

Table 3.2 Chapters of the accession negotiations

1	Free movement of goods
2	Free movement of persons
3	Freedom to provide services
4	Free movement of capital
5	Company law
6	Competition policy
7	Agriculture
8	Fisheries
9	Transport policy
10	Taxation
11	Economic and Monetary Union
12	Statistics
13	Social policy and employment
14	Energy
15	Industrial policy
16	Small and medium-sized enterprises
17	Science and research
18	Education and training
19	Telecommunications and information technologies
20	Culture and audio-visual policy
21	Regional policy and coordination of structural instruments
22	Environment
23	Consumers and health protection
24	Cooperation in the field of justice and home affairs
25	Customs union
26	External relations
27	Common foreign and security policy
28	Financial control
29	Financial and budgetary provisions
30	Institutions
31	Other

'Budget' (the payments of new members into the EU's budget) and 'Institutions' (their allocation of votes and seats in the EU's policy-making bodies). The last chapter 'Other' provides a place for matters not directly related to the *acquis*, or which cannot easily be placed in other chapters. It may be noted that in the preceding accession negotiations of 1993–4 there were only 29 chapters: the increase to 31 was due partly to intervening changes in EU policies – for example, Financial Control became an independent chapter because of the importance now accorded to it.

Main stages of the negotiations

The accession negotiations of 1998–2003 can be divided into five main phases:

- An initial stage of 'screening' of the *acquis* (April to November 1998).
- The opening of 'easy' chapters with six countries (November 1998 to January 2000).

- The extension of the negotiations to include six more countries, and the opening of more chapters (February to December 2000).
- A phase of acceleration resulting from the introduction of the 'road-map' and the definition of EU positions for most chapters (January to December 2001).
- The final phase, with discussion of the budget-related chapters, leading to political agreement at Copenhagen and the text of the Treaty (January 2001 to February 2002).

The following sections summarise events in chronological order, with an explanation of the problems encountered in the main chapters. Such a summary is inevitably selective, and in a short space it not possible to discuss all the chapters or the positions of all the countries concerned.

The initial phase: screening of the *acquis*

After the formal opening of the negotiations, the first practical step was the 'screening' exercise, more correctly described as the 'analytical examination of the *acquis*'. This was a technical but necessary preliminary phase in which, as in the accession negotiations of 1993–4, the Commission scrutinised with the applicant countries the whole of the EU legislation in force, estimated at 80,000 pages of the *Official Journal*. The aim was to ensure that they fully understood their future obligations as members and to identify potential issues for the negotiations. Because of the wish of the EU for assurances that the new members would effectively transpose and apply EU rules, the screening of 1998, unlike that of 1993, included an examination of the planned timetables of the applicant countries for applying the *acquis*. This emphasised from the outset the link between the negotiations and the pre-accession strategy.

The screening meetings, unlike the negotiations proper, were conducted by the Commission with the applicant countries collectively, but in two separate groups consisting of the six countries already in negotiations, and the others. At least, that was the case for the 'didactic' sessions of the screening, which were followed by bilateral sessions in which the countries explained individually to the Commission where they would have problems. As new *acquis* developed, the screening process continued at regular intervals throughout the negotiations.

The opening of easy chapters

Reports on the screening were made by the Commission to the Council in autumn 1998, leading to the EU's decision to open seven chapters in the negotiations. The chapters chosen were 'easy' ones such as Statistics, in which the *acquis* presented no difficulties and the applicant countries were expected to have few problems. Meanwhile they were asked to submit 'position papers' stating their requests. At this stage, the negotiations consisted of the applicant countries stating whether they could accept the *acquis* fully on accession, or requesting transitional periods, to which the Commission proposed appropriate responses for the EU side; these responses were often negative and the Commission sometimes persuaded the applicants to withdraw requests before discussion of them in the conference.

As the negotiations continued into 1999, more chapters were opened and a number of easier ones were closed, in which the applicants agreed to apply the *acquis* fully on accession. Frustration began to be voiced by the applicants, who felt that the pace was too slow and the conduct of the conferences was too formal, with no real exchange of views. This was linked to apprehension that the negotiations would be delayed because of the EU's need to take important decisions on its future financial framework (decided at Berlin in March 1999 on the basis of the Commission's Agenda 2000 proposals) and on its institutional reform (decided at Nice in December 2000).

The extension of the negotiations to more countries

When the negotiations opened it was understood that they could be extended to other applicant countries and in the second half of 1999 it began to be accepted that this would be the case. Following a change of government in September 1998, Malta had reactivated its application for membership and in February 1999 the Commission, in a revised Opinion, recommended the opening of the screening exercise and later negotiations with Malta. A change of government in Slovakia in September 1998 led to a new political situation in which this country fulfilled the political criterion for membership – the only problem that had prevented it from opening negotiations already. Latvia and Lithuania, which unlike their neighbour Estonia had not been considered in 1997 as fulfilling sufficiently the criteria for membership, had been spurred on in the meantime to make better progress. For Bulgaria and Romania, which still lagged behind the others, the EU felt sympathy because of the economic difficulties which they were suffering as a result of the conflict in Kosovo.

In its reports in October 1999 the Commission accordingly recommended bringing the six other applicant countries into the accession negotiations, and after approval by the European Council at Helsinki in December 1999, these countries (the Helsinki group) commenced negotiations with a series of ministerial meetings on 15 February 2000.

This development added to the concern of the first six countries (the Luxembourg group) about the risks of delay. Although 23 of the 31 chapters had been formally opened for negotiation by the end of 1999 and between nine and ten of them had been closed with different countries, there was no real negotiation yet on any of the difficult issues. In the early months of

2000 the applicants began to voice complaints that the EU was failing to confront the issues and being 'evasive' in the negotiations, in which its positions sometimes took the form of further questions, rather than replies to the requests of the applicants. In the field of agriculture, for example, the EU's position papers were silent on the important question of direct payments to farmers in the new member states, for which a position would be taken 'at a later stage'.

For the six countries that commenced in 1998, the opening of chapters was perceived as an index of progress in the negotiations. In the absence of negotiations on politically important matters, interest tended to focus on the formal situation of the number of chapters opened and closed with each country, for which a 'score-sheet' was regularly published in the press. With the arrival of six more countries, some of which were able to catch up rapidly, the 'score-sheets' of chapters opened and closed assumed a higher profile. For the members of the Luxembourg group, it even seemed that 'catching-up' by the members of the Helsinki group in the negotiations was an objective on the part of the EU.

Despite efforts by the Commission to relativise this 'football-league' approach, it tended to dominate the reports of sessions of the conferences. Superficially it gave a tactical advantage to the EU, by putting the applicant countries under pressure to accept EU positions and thus close chapters, but it also tended to obscure the important message that progress towards membership depended on good preparation 'on the ground' rather than negotiations in Brussels. This accent on progress with chapters – an activity which was ironically dubbed 'chapterology' – was especially artificial in the case of Bulgaria and Romania, whose preparation for membership lagged behind the others.

The closure of chapters in the negotiations was at this stage only 'provisional': not only did each side reserve the right to reopen chapters later, either because of the well-established principle of negotiations that 'nothing is agreed until everything is agreed', or because of the possibility of new problems resulting from the introduction of new *acquis*, but the EU also reserved the right to reopen chapters if an applicant country failed to keep its engagements concerning the application of the *acquis*. In this way, the link was maintained between the negotiations and the process of domestic preparation, on which the Commission made periodic monitoring reports. Although the threat to reopen chapters for this reason was occasionally made, it was sufficiently effective not to need execution.

The battle of the dates

In the course of 2000 the question of the timetable for completing negotiations and the date of accession began, more and more, to preoccupy the applicant countries, particularly those who considered themselves to be well prepared for membership. Discussion of the date of enlargement had been politically active for a number of years, with the applicants hoping for a target date for enlargement from the EU and the EU refusing to commit itself.

An earlier round in this 'battle of the dates' had taken place in 1997, when the Commission decided in its Opinions to base its assessment of the applicant countries' readiness for membership on a prospective 'medium-term' horizon of five years, using the year 2002 as a 'working hypothesis' for accession. This was already a disappointment for some applicant countries, who considered that German Chancellor Kohl and French President Chirac had signalled to Poland that 2000 would be its date of entry.

However, as the applicants began to make concrete plans for introducing the *acquis*, even 2002 began to appear ambitious and by the time that negotiations opened in 1998 Poland and others were basing their accession plans on 2003, with only Hungary retaining 2002 as the year when it would be ready. These plans, which were examined in the screening exercise, were important for the negotiations from a tactical point of view, since it was in relation to their 'self-selected' dates of accession that each country made requests for transitional periods.

For its part, the EU refused for a long time to be drawn into precision on the date of accession, relying on the Delphic formula that the Union would be ready to welcome new members 'from 2002 onwards'. It remained deaf to the pleas of the applicants, particularly Poland, to fix a target date for accession as a means of accelerating the adoption of the *acquis* by the applicants. Realists on the EU side considered that a target date would be interpreted as a promise, thus relaxing rather than reinforcing the pressure for good preparation.

Nevertheless, as the negotiations progressed and more important chapters began to be closed, the question was naturally posed as to when all the chapters could be closed. The applicants continued to press for a timetable, arguing that the technique of dates and deadlines was a traditional way for reaching decisions within the EU; for example, already in October 1999 and again in June and November 2000, the foreign ministers of the Luxembourg group had urged the EU to accelerate the negotiations, and conclude them in the course of 2001.

Although the Council was reluctant to move towards a timetable, the Commission and the Parliament indicated certain parameters. Taking office as president of the Commission in September 1999, Romano Prodi declared that one of his main aims was to achieve the first accessions before the end of the Commission's mandate, due to expire in January 2005. The new Commissioner for Enlargement, Guenter Verheugen, said in September 1999 that 2004 was 'the most reasonable and realistic date for the first accessions'. Then in the autumn of 2000 the parliament voted in favour of the new members acceding in time to take part in its next elections, due to take place in June 2004.

The question of the first wave

Reflection on when enlargement would take place was inevitably linked to speculation as to which countries would be included. Some member states, such as Austria, argued for a rapid 'first wave' of enlargement with a small group of well-prepared countries, even as few as three, on the grounds that this would ease the way for later accessions, whereas a big first wave taking in most of the twelve countries could be subject to delay. Those applicants who were most confident of their good preparation, such as Hungary, Slovenia and Estonia, gave quiet support to the idea and commentators saw Poland at risk of being left out because of alleged shortcomings in its preparation. Poland was believed in some quarters to have obtained an assurance from its neighbour Germany that it would be included in a first wave; although the Poles denied playing such a 'political card', they nevertheless argued that a first wave without them would lose much of its political value, since Poland with 39 million inhabitants was by far the biggest applicant country of central Europe.

By the autumn of 2000 the press was speculating on a so-called 'big-bang' scenario with the accession of up to ten countries in 2005 or 2006. Meanwhile the Commission resolutely maintained that it was premature to predict which countries would be ready, and that the choice would be made on objective criteria – with no 'political discount' for any country.

The European Council at Feira in June 2000, which pledged to 'maintain the momentum' of the negotiations, was a disappointment to the applicants, who had hoped for a commitment to a 'qualitatively new phase'. The presidency for the second half of 2000 (France) began to talk of introducing a 'road-map', described as a 'scenario without dates', in the negotiations, but it was unclear what this might mean. Attention now began to be focused increasingly on the intergovernmental conference which was to reach agreement by the end of the year on institutional reforms for enlargement; although the accession negotiations continued to make modest progress, there was apprehension that a failure to reach agreement at the European Council in Nice might cause a long delay in enlargement.

The road-map

At this point, the Commission introduced a new element with a decisive influence on the progress of the accession negotiations. Together with its regular reports in November 2000, it issued a Strategy Paper recommending a 'road-map', in essence, a timetable for completing the negotiations, chapter by chapter, by the end of 2002. What the Commission proposed was for the EU to commit itself to complete its common positions for all the chapters and present them to the applicant countries, progressively over the next three periods of six months, thus spreading the timetable over three successive presidencies of the Council.

For the applicant countries this gave more precision concerning the timetable and an assurance that the EU would now complete its positions (which in some important areas were vague or non-existent); it also gave the hope – though not the guarantee – that the chapters could be closed within the same time-frame. For the EU side it provided the discipline to take decisions on difficult aspects of the negotiations and also served as a powerful incentive for successive presidencies to make achievement of the timetable a criterion of their success. Although there was some 'slippage' on the EU side, particularly in the first half of 2002, the road-map effectively ensured that the negotiations concluded within the next two years. Within the Commission it also provided a necessary discipline, for the task of preparing proposals for difficult chapters of the negotiation required important technical and political input from the various Commissioners and services responsible.

The road-map gave no indication of the date of enlargement, simply stating that negotiations could be concluded 'by the end of 2002' with countries that had made sufficient progress by that time. This prudently left the second half of 2002, following the formal completion of the road-map, for the finalisation of the negotiations. When the Council gave its agreement to this plan in December 2000, Guenter Verheugen declared it to be 'the best day since he came to office'.

Decisions at Nice

At the European Council in Nice in December 2000 agreement was also reached – after difficult discussions – on institutional reforms for enlargement. The role of the applicant countries in these discussions was limited: they had no voice in the intergovernmental conference, but they hoped to obtain equitable treatment, that is a representation equal to that of EU members of similar size. Even this required energetic diplomatic efforts, including telephone calls to Nice, where some member states, intent on the internal struggle within EU-15, were inclined to ignore the interests of the newcomers. The final result was not equitable for Hungary and the Czech Republic, whose allocation of seats in the European Parliament was less than for existing members of similar population such as Belgium and Portugal.

Political disputes at Nice, particularly between bigger and smaller members, projected a poor image of the EU and many considered that the results fell far below the initial hopes for institutional reform. Nevertheless, the fact that agreement was reached was a great relief for the applicant countries, for it opened the way for further progress in the negotiations. Thus at the beginning of 2001 a new dynamism was given to the enlargement process. For the first half of the year the Commission's road-map called for decisions on some important chapters, particularly Environment, Free Movement of Persons and Free Movement of Capital.

The 'environment' chapter

It was evident before the negotiations began that the new members would need long transitional periods to implement parts of the EU's environmental policy. Many environmental standards in central and eastern Europe were below those in the West and compliance with the *acquis* would require costly investments in infrastructure and technology in both public and private sectors. In fact, the EU had needed transitional periods for its own members to introduce these rules. On the other hand, business circles in the EU argued that exceptions for the new members would give them an unfair competitive advantage in the single market.

Potentially this could have been one of the most difficult chapters in the negotiations, for long transitional periods of ten years or more were requested and the Commission was initially resistant. However, in the course of the negotiations it began to be recognised that a distinction could be made between the 'product-related' aspects of the environmental rules and other areas that would have little or no impact on the single market, such as standards for drinking water. On this basis, agreement was reached with Slovenia, one of the most environment-conscious of the applicant countries, on a series of transitional periods, allowing the chapter to be closed with Slovenia in March 2001 and then in June 2001 with Hungary, the Czech Republic and Estonia. This set a pattern for the resolution of the Environment chapter with the others and effectively defused a problem which could have been a complicating factor in the final stages of the negotiations.

The 'free movement of persons' chapter

This also was an area where difficulties were anticipated. For Germany and Austria the admission to their labour market of workers from the adjacent countries of central Europe was a sensitive political issue, in view of domestic unemployment and lower wage-levels in countries such as Poland. Although the free movement of persons is one of the 'four freedoms' of the EU's single market, it was excluded from the Europe Agreements. The applicant countries expected that the EU would propose some kind of transitional arrangement; and since the negotiations up to now had consisted exclusively of requests by the applicants for transitional periods, such a request from the EU would create a new tactical situation, particularly since the EU had insisted on the single market as a key area of the *acquis* in which the applicants should apply all the rules on accession.

Within the EU opinions were divided on the need for such an arrangement. The member states geographically distant from the newcomers in central Europe did not share the apprehensions of Germany and Austria, which they considered to be exaggerated, particularly at a time when increased labour mobility was becoming a central theme of the EU's employment policy and demographic studies showed a need for the EU to import more manpower in the medium and long term. Although a seven-year transitional period for free movement of workers had been agreed for the accession of Spain and Portugal in 1985, that was before the creation of the single market with free movement as one of its principles. Plainly the applicant countries would have good grounds to resist if the EU asked for an exception in this area and would try to extract a price for it – possibly a budgetary price – in the negotiations.

The Commission was thus faced with a difficult choice in this chapter. Already in May 2000 a detailed economic study, carried out at the Commission's request, had concluded that the threat of migration of workers from the new members was exaggerated. The problem was essentially political – how to reassure the public in Germany and Austria, particularly in the border regions, that enlargement would not result in an uncontrolled influx of workers. In April 2001 Guenter Verheugen took a bold and successful initiative, bringing forward a proposal for a flexible transitional period under which the 15 EU member states could each decide for themselves whether to maintain restrictions on workers from the new members for a period of up to seven years.

The reaction from the applicant countries was strong. Their public opinion was unhappy at the idea of having to wait for a long time before enjoying what was seen as one of the main benefits of membership – the right to work elsewhere in the EU. The proposal was perceived as a form of 'second-class membership'. There was irritation that it was formulated in an identical way for all the central European countries, without taking account of their individual situations. Countries such as the Czech Republic and Slovenia felt that the smaller wage-gap between them and the EU should be taken into account; Estonia argued that with its small population it posed no threat to other labour markets; Hungary came with a counter-proposal for the EU to analyse the problem separately with each applicant. Some of the countries, who felt that they were being asked to pay a collective price for a problem that mainly concerned Poland, saw the handling of this chapter as a test-case for the principle of differentiation, and were frustrated that the EU ignored their arguments.

At this juncture Spain tabled a memorandum on regional policy, referring to the problems posed for Spanish regions by enlargement and this initiative was interpreted in the press as a tactical move, threatening to deny satisfaction to Germany and Austria in the chapter concerning free movement of workers unless Spain's concerns in another chapter were recognised. Although such a link was denied by Spain, which accepted that its problem would be examined in another context, the incident raised the temperature on the EU side and gave a foretaste of possible difficulties of linkage of chapters in the negotiations. However, the Council soon accepted the Commission's seven-year proposal, which was presented to the applicant countries in June 2001 and was accepted by Hungary, Slovakia and Latvia.

In October 2001 it was accepted also by the Czech Republic, but with the addition of a clause allowing the Czechs to limit workers from the other new members. It is interesting to note that this improvement obtained by the Czechs was automatically extended to the other applicants, even though some of them had already closed the chapter – an acceptance by the EU that a concession to one country could not be denied to others. Poland, significantly, from the point of view of its tactics in the negotiations at this stage, refused to accept the seven-year proposal.

It should be explained here that the deal on 'free movement of persons' was in the context of the single market – concerning the right of citizens to take up employment in other member states – and not in the context of the Schengen rules – the right to pass internal EU frontiers without submitting to identity controls. Citizens of the new member states will not obtain the latter until they join the Schengen area, some time after accession.

The agreement at this stage on free movement of workers had several important consequences. First, it helped to defuse a political problem in Germany and Austria, and avoided enlargement becoming a divisive issue in Germany's elections. Second, it led to a more realistic and sympathetic attitude on the EU side to requests from the applicants. Previously, the EU had been very restrictive on transitional periods; now it was more ready to accept that the immediate application of the *acquis* could pose economic and political problems for the applicants, as it had done for some EU members. From this point of view, the agreement on a relatively long period of up to seven years to deal with a problem on the EU side represented a psychological turning-point in the negotiations.

The 'free movement of capital' chapter: agricultural land

A number of the applicant countries wished to control purchase of property by foreigners, particularly agricultural land, after accession, and proposed long transitional periods for this purpose: Poland requested 18 years, and Hungary, the Czech Republic and Slovakia 10 years for restrictions on agricultural property.

They argued that the much lower prices of property in their countries, as a result of lower incomes and lower levels of agricultural support, would encourage an influx of foreign buyers from richer EU members such as Germany. Since such transactions are covered by EU rules on free movement of capital, the request was handled in that chapter.

Free movement of capital, like free movement of workers, is one of the 'four freedoms' of the single market and moreover the nature of the problem presented by the applicants for agricultural land had similarities to that presented by the EU for workers: fear of an uncontrolled influx of foreigners resulting from the difference in levels of economic development. It was not surprising therefore that in April 2001 the Commission proposed a seven-year transitional period also for free movement of capital, as it had for free movement of workers, and in June this position was presented to the applicants.

The acceleration of the negotiations

By mid-2001 it was clear that, as a result of the road-map, the negotiations were moving into a higher gear. The EU had demonstrated its engagement by taking positions on some important chapters, though not yet on the key 'budget-related' questions. As a result, the applicant countries were now under more pressure, faced with a situation in which they had to react to EU proposals on politically important matters and to competition between themselves. Hungary was seen to be pursuing a strategy of rapid and constructive response to EU positions, seeking to close chapters on realistic terms and providing a model for others to follow (although the others felt that Hungary was sometimes too rapid). Poland, on the other hand, was perceived to be resisting EU positions in a number of chapters and hoping to obtain better terms by resisting pressure. However, at this time Poland had a minority government facing impending elections and the concessions necessary to reach agreement would have required an abrupt turn-about in positions which their negotiators had optimistically declared in public, thus raising domestic expectations.

Meanwhile the debate continued, in public and in private, on the date of enlargement and the countries to be included in a 'first wave'. In June 2001 the European Council in Gothenburg confirmed that it should be possible to conclude negotiations by the end of 2002, although some EU members initially resisted this formula. Press reports suggested that the hesitation was partly due to a fear that a deadline would undermine the substance of the negotiations and partly by German doubts that Poland would be ready in time. It was certainly the case that at this stage Poland, normally the most vigorous in demanding a date for conclusion, was lagging behind in the negotiations.

Interest intensified in the relative positions of the applicant countries as indicated by the 'score-sheet'. Some of the countries of the Helsinki group had caught up with the Luxembourg group: by mid-June Poland had closed 16 chapters while Hungary and Cyprus, with 22 chapters closed, were now the 'front-runners'.

Concerning the number of countries to be included in a first wave, speculation increased that it could be as many as ten. In February 2001 the Budget Commissioner Michaele Schreyer stated that under the EU's financial framework for the period up to 2006 there was room for ten new members (the agreement on the budget at Berlin had envisaged only six accessions in 2002). This formula was taken up in the Commission's strategy paper in November 2001, which referred to the possibility of 'up to ten countries' acceding in 2004. Although the Commission's regular reports on the applicant countries gave no explicit ranking of countries, it was clear which ten were under consideration for accession since Bulgaria and Romania were lagging behind in pre-accession preparation, as well as in the accession negotiations.

A remark of France's foreign minister at this stage gave rise to fresh speculation about the future scenario. He commented to the press that if enlargement were to be a political process, it would be desirable to include Bulgaria and Romania. Although this was seen by some as an indication that France wished to delay enlargement, others saw it as a warning that Poland should not count on being included in a first wave on 'political' grounds.

The preparation of the final stage: the Laeken group

A decisive step was taken at Laeken, Belgium, in December 2001 when the European Council not only confirmed that negotiations could be concluded with up to ten countries by the end of 2002, provided that satisfactory progress continued, but also listed them as Cyprus, Estonia, Hungary, Latvia, Lithuania, Malta, Poland, the Slovak Republic, the Czech Republic and Slovenia.

The definition of this 'Laeken group' of countries signalled the end of the distinction between Luxembourg and Helsinki groups, and opened the way for the final phase of negotiations. Although the 'road-map' had led the EU to take positions in the course of 2001 on the majority of chapters, it had left over until the first half of 2002 the budget-related chapters: the Budget chapter itself – concerning the new members' payments into the EU budget – and the main policies under which they would obtain receipts from it – the Agriculture and Regional Policy chapters.

It had been possible to handle other chapters in the negotiations more or less independently of the question as to when enlargement would take place and which countries would be included in it. But for concrete negotiations on expenditure, within budgetary limits, it was necessary to be more precise. From this point of view the definition of the Laeken group facilitated the opening of budgetary matters by defusing the question of who would be included in the first round.

Meanwhile Poland, after a change of government, had effectively caught up with the other countries in terms of the number of chapters closed; in November 2001 it accepted the EU's seven-year transitional period for free movement of workers and in January 2002 the Commission signalled that it could accept the Polish request for 12 years for acquisition of agricultural land. Now, with between 20 and 25 chapters closed by all members of the Laeken group, the 'score-sheet' became less important and competition between countries became less intense. As the main remaining problems centred on the budget-related chapters, it became evident that a 'package deal' covering all ten countries would be the last and most difficult part of the negotiations.

In this context, the applicant countries and the EU tended to view Poland as the critical actor since its size (39 million, compared with 36 million for the other nine countries combined) meant that whatever was decided for it would have a decisive effect on the contours of the overall package. The other applicants began to let Poland 'take the strain' in the negotiations, watching carefully to see what it obtained.

The financial package

The Commission addressed the last big problem by taking an initiative in January 2002 on the financial arrangements for the period 2004–6. Its memorandum effectively defined the framework for the rest of the negotiations, since although the EU's common position was not defined until October, leaving only six weeks for 'official' negotiations with the applicant countries, the existence of the proposal served from January onwards to identify the key financial issues and to set the parameters for their solution. It ensured that discussion of the three financial chapters was well co-ordinated and increased pressure to resolve other non-financial issues in the meantime.

The Commission's proposal, based on the hypothesis that ten new members would join on 1 January 2004, concerned the period 2004–6, the first three years of their membership. The limitation to this period was necessary because the EU's budgetary deal at Berlin in 1999 related to the period 2000–6 and, in the absence of an *acquis* concerning the subsequent period, the payments and receipts of the new members after 2006 could not be discussed in the accession negotiations. The fact that the short-term and longer-term budgetary consequences of enlargement were thus so clearly separated was an important factor of simplification: if the accession negotiations had included, or been accompanied by, a negotiation of the EU's future receipts and expenditure, they could not have been concluded in 2002.

For the period 2004–6 the Commission envisaged expenditure of 40.16 billion euros for the ten new members in terms of 'commitment appropriations'. Compared with the Berlin agreement, this was less than the amount provided for 2004–6, but more than the amount provided for the years 2002–4 which according to the original hypothesis would have been the first three years of enlargement with six countries: thus the volume proposed was justified by the postponement of enlargement to a later date, but with more countries involved.

Of the 40.16 billion euros, 64 per cent was destined for structural expenditure (essentially, regional policy), 24 per cent for agriculture, and 12 per cent for other EU expenditure. Meanwhile the new members were to pay their full contributions to the EU budget from accession onwards – unlike Greece, Spain and Portugal, which had obtained a 'phasing-in' – but to avoid the risk of their becoming net contributors to the budget, the

Commission proposed an additional reserve of 2.43 billion euros for 'budgetary compensation'. In fact, the declared aim was to ensure that the net receipts of new members after accession should not be less than their receipts from pre-accession funds in the year before enlargement. This was the fundamental principle that guided the construction and development of the EU's budgetary package: that the receipts of the new members should not decrease as a result of accession.

The applicant countries reacted immediately by describing the proposals as inadequate. Not only did they fall below the amounts provided by Berlin for 2004–6, but they were perceived as unfair: in the field of regional policy they represented only 137 euros per head of population for the new members in 2006, compared with 231 euros per head for Greece, Spain and Portugal and in the field of agriculture they were based on a phasing-in of the EU's scheme of 'direct payments' to farmers commencing at 25 per cent in 2004 and rising to 100 per cent over a long transitional period of ten years. The reaction of some EU members was the opposite: they argued that the total amount should be lower (nearer to the total provided by Berlin for 2002–4) and that (in conformity with Berlin) there should be no 'direct payments' for the new members.

The 'agriculture' chapter: direct payments

In view of the importance which this agricultural problem assumed in the negotiations, it needs to be explained in more detail. In 1997 when it gave its Opinions on the applicant countries, the Commission already identified the 'direct payments' scheme, introduced in 1990 to compensate EU farmers for a reform of the common agricultural policy, as a potential difficulty of enlargement. It would be so expensive to apply to the CEECs, with their large number of farmers, that it would overshoot the EU's budgetary limits. Moreover, it was argued that agriculture in the new member countries, which had not experienced the EU's reform, did not need such compensation, and that the payment of large sums to individual farmers in these countries would slow down the improvement of their farm structure.

The Commission advocated that direct payments should not be available to farmers in the acceding countries and consequently they were excluded from the calculation of the EU's budgetary deal in Berlin. The weakness in this argument, however, was that direct payments continued to be paid to farmers in the EU long after the reforms and were part of the agricultural *acquis*, which the EU was urging the applicant countries to apply in all other respects. The applicants emphasised continuously, from the start of the negotiations, that as a matter of principle the agricultural policy should be applied to them under equal conditions.

Despite what had been agreed at Berlin, the Commission concluded by 2002 that a proposal which included no direct payments would be difficult to reconcile with the EU's principle of no modification of the *acquis* and would be politically unacceptable for the applicant countries. Therefore it proposed a long transitional period. Meanwhile some EU members such as France began to take a more favourable view of the inclusion of the payments, realising that the refusal of them to farmers in the new members would strengthen the pressure from countries such as Germany and Britain to abolish them altogether in the EU.

The 'institutions' chapter

Soon after the Commission's financial proposal it became clear that, despite the road-map's promise of EU positions on all budget-related chapters in the first half of 2002, agreement within the EU on the overall financial package was unlikely until after the German elections in September. So progress continued with other chapters.

In April the EU defined its position on the Institutions chapter, concerning the seats and votes of new members in the European institutions such as Parliament, Council and Commission. It contained no surprises, being largely based on decisions already taken by the EU in Nice and was soon accepted by a number of countries – with the exception of Hungary and the Czech Republic, which continued to argue for more seats in the European Parliament to bring them into line with other countries of similar size. This request was finally satisfied in the last stage of the negotiations through the redistribution of seats allocated at Nice for Bulgaria and Romania.

Among other things, the Institutions chapter provided for the official languages of the EU institutions to be increased from 11 to 20, taking account of the languages of all the acceding countries, including the 'smallest' language Maltese; moreover, Turkish would also need to be added in the event of a political solution in Cyprus.

Other chapters

In other chapters of the negotiations there were important and difficult discussions, sometimes leading to agreement on transitional periods and sometimes of concern to a limited number of countries, which cannot be described in a summary of this kind. For example, there were negotiations in the fields of pharmaceuticals, state aids, many aspects of the implementation of the agricultural policy, transport (including 'cabotage', the right of road hauliers from one country to carry goods between places in another country), taxation (for food, spirits, heating, cigarettes, fuels, construction, etc.), energy and so on.

In some important chapters, the negotiations had nothing to do with transitional periods or requests of the applicant countries but with the confirmation that they could and would apply the *acquis*, particularly in the field of justice and home affairs where the plans of each country for implementing the Schengen system of border controls were clarified. It is interesting to note that, for the control of persons at internal borders, the application of the *acquis* itself requires a decision to be taken only later, after enlargement, on the date when the new members can join the Schengen zone. In a similar way, in the field of Economic and Monetary Union, it follows from the *acquis* that they will not join the eurozone on accession, but later when they fulfil the necessary conditions including the 'Maastricht criteria'.

In the case of the CFSP chapter, there was no question of transitional periods and no need for negotiation, since the applicants subscribed unreservedly to the *acquis* in this area, with which they had been cooperating actively for some time. Although they tend to have a more 'Atlanticist' outlook than some member states – as the Iraq crisis in 2003 demonstrated – such a question had no place in the accession negotiations.

By the end of the negotiations it was estimated that a total of 322 transitional measures (mainly for the ten applicant countries, but also for the EU) had been agreed in 17 of the 31 chapters. Of these, about two-thirds were concentrated in the chapters concerning Agriculture (73), Taxation (59), Environment (56) and the first four chapters relating to the single market (43). No transitional measures were found to be necessary in 14 chapters where the acquis will be applied fully on accession: Company Law, Fisheries, Economic and Monetary Union, Statistics, Industry, Small and Medium-sized Enterprises, Science and Research, Education and Training, Regional Policy, Consumers and Health Protection, Justice and Home Affairs, External Relations, Common and Foreign Security Policy, Financial Control, Budget.

The end game

As the applicant countries waited for the EU to finalise its financial proposals, their perceptions and positions on some aspects of the package began to shift. They now tended to accept the Commission's basic proposal for Regional Policy, under which the total amount available would be distributed to the ten countries according to a pre-determined scale. In the agriculture chapter, they began to signal that they could accept a transitional period for direct payments, but still sought better terms; Poland, for example, said that it could accept three years (not ten years) if the starting-point was higher. Technical discussions were also now under way on the other aspects of the agriculture chapter, such as quotas and reference quantities, for which they sought higher amounts.

Meanwhile it began to be accepted by the EU that the applicants were justified in arguing that the credits for 'payments' – the actual receipts of the new members – would be so much lower than the credits for 'appropriations' that there was a real risk of their having a negative cash-flow in the early years of membership. In September the Commission estimated that, unless adjustments were made, the package could result in six new members obtaining lower net receipts in 2004 than in 2003 and four of them would be net contributors to the EU budget. In October the finance ministers of the ten countries issued a joint statement demanding a solution to this problem through the phasing-in of their contributions to the EU budget.

There was now a series of developments on the EU side, which allowed the 'end-game' of the negotiations to commence. In September the Irish people removed a potential road-block to enlargement by voting 'yes' in a second referendum on the Treaty of Nice, the first referendum having given a 'no' in June 2001. The Commission in its regular reports in October concluded that the ten countries of the Laeken group would be ready for membership 'from the beginning of 2004'. The European Council in Brussels endorsed this view and agreed, at last, on an overall financial package for the negotiations amounting to a total of 39.23 billion euros for the period 2004–6; compared with the Commission's initial proposal, this represented a reduction of 2 billion euros in Structural Funds.

With the presentation of this package by the Danish presidency to the applicant countries on 28 October 2002, the last frenetic round commenced. At this stage the EU side insisted that while the total amount could not be increased, there might be flexibility on the 'non-financial' issues. At a joint meeting in Warsaw in mid-November the prime ministers of the ten countries declared that there should either be a phasing-in of their payments, or a 'compensatory mechanism' for the budget and they continued to oppose the EU's position on direct payments for agriculture.

After a meeting between the foreign ministers of the applicant countries and their EU counterparts on 18 November, the presidency took an important initiative in launching on 25 November a compromise package which increased the amount for 2004–6 by 1.3 billion euros and allowed the new members to 'top up' the 'direct payments' in agriculture by switching some budgetary resources from 'rural development' (a concession sought particularly by the Poles). At the same time, the EU decided that the date of enlargement should be 1 May rather than 1 January 2004; although this delay of four months was justified by the need to allow more time for ratification of enlargement, it had another important consequence for the negotiations. Since the new members would pay less into the budget for 2004 (payments for only eight months) but obtain receipts for the full year, this ingenious device helped to solve the 'cash-flow' problem for the first year of membership.

Agreement at Copenhagen

After bilateral meetings with the applicant countries in early December 2002, the EU approved (retrospectively) the compromise package proposed by the presidency and the scene was set for an encounter with them at the level of prime ministers at the European Council in Copenhagen on 12–13

December. Here the presidency skilfully organised further bilateral meetings, making concessions such as further flexibility for the 'topping-up' of the direct payments in agriculture to 55 per cent in the first year and added a final budgetary concession in the form of a 'Schengen facility' and additional budgetary compensation. This last move increased the total amount for 2004–6 for the new members to 40.85 billion euros.

Several applicant countries signalled their readiness to accept this approach and when it was agreed with Poland, the deal was effectively done. The conclusion of the negotiations was announced to the press as an achievement which 'testifies to the common determination of the peoples of Europe to come together in a Union that has become the driving force for peace, democracy, stability and prosperity on our continent'. Thus, at Copenhagen in December 2002 the EU fulfilled the historic promise that it made to the central and east European countries ten years earlier at Copenhagen.

Finalisation and signature of the treaty

Although the main problems of the negotiations were resolved, it still remained to put the results into legal form in a treaty of accession. This task occupied negotiators of both sides in Brussels for the next few weeks until the EU finally agreed the text on 5 February 2003. The treaty itself is rather short – just three articles, listing the acceding countries and giving the date of accession – while the annexed Act of Accession is a much larger document, composed of five parts, nine protocols, 44 declarations, numerous exchanges of letters, and 18 annexes. Annex 2 is the longest, containing most of the 'technical adaptations' to EU legislation necessary for the accession of the new members.

The complete set of documents is the most voluminous in the history of the EU: it exists in 21 languages, each occupying 1,000 pages in the format of the *Official Journal*, but up to 5,000 pages in more normal format.

The treaty was transmitted to the European Parliament in February for examination and on 9 April it gave its assent by a large majority. Then, on 16 April, it was signed in Athens by high-level representatives of the 25 contracting parties (15 member states and ten acceding countries). Ratification is due to be made according to the constitutional requirements of each country, with referendums held in nine of the acceding countries.

Assessment

What comments can be made on the accession negotiations and the enlargement process? Other chapters of this book discuss wider issues such as the attitude of the new members to European integration and the impact of enlargement on the politics and economics of the European Union. These remarks focus on the following questions: the length of the process leading to the enlargement in 2004 (was it too long, or not long enough?), and the results of the negotiations (how satisfactory were they for the parties concerned?).

Length of the accession process

In the 'battle of dates' for enlargement, the applicant countries often saw the position of the EU as a means of delay. Repeated calls for a timetable received no concrete response from the EU until the end of 2000, with the introduction of the 'road-map', which implied the end of negotiations in 2002 and (probably) accession in 2004. Indeed, the first to fix the important parameter that enlargement should take place by mid-2004 in time for the European elections was the European Parliament – an institution with no official part in the negotiations.

On the EU side there was always a commitment to enlargement: the promise made at Copenhagen in 1993 was repeatedly confirmed by the European Council and no EU leader took positions that could be interpreted as blocking the process of eastern enlargement. The question on the EU side was not whether enlargement should take place, but how and when. But the 'when' and 'how' were difficult problems, with a continuing fear in many quarters that the applicant countries had not made sufficient progress in preparation to apply the EU rules and policies. Most important, the key factor in ensuring a good preparation was the conditionality of the accession process: as soon as the EU gave a precise timetable, it knew that it would lose a large part of its 'leverage'.

The hesitations on the EU side, even at the end of the negotiations, were demonstrated by the 'safeguard clauses', of wider scope than in previous enlargements, that were included in the accession treaty. These safeguard clauses allow for 'protective measures' to be taken in the three years following enlargement in the areas of economy, internal market, and justice and home affairs; these measures can be triggered by difficulties or failure to implement commitments in the new member states. It remains to be seen whether these clauses will be invoked, or (as generally happened in the past) will simply serve as a reassurance.

It has been suggested that enlargement in 2004 is premature and that a few more years of preparation would ensure a better result, not only in terms of implementation of EU policies by the new members but also of reform of the EU. But the reality is that by 2002 the benefits of conditionality had reached their political limits: for nearly a decade, the applicant countries had shown patience and understanding of the EU's wish for adequate preparation but expectations on their side had reached the point where more waiting could have been counter-productive. Compared with their self-selected timetables for implementing the *acquis* by 2002 or 2003, accession in 2004 represented a small but acceptable (even expected) delay: to postpone it further could have undermined their political will for better preparation.

On the EU side too, the timing of the conclusion of the negotiations and of enlargement itself was optimal in relation to its overall political calendar: with its decisions at Berlin on the budget for 2004–6, the EU was able to accept enlargement in 2004 without becoming involved at the same time in the difficult question of the post-2006 budgetary framework, which would have led to much delay. Enlargement in 2005 or 2006, for example, would have been more difficult to manage.

From these points of view, the duration of the enlargement process must surely be considered as neither too long nor too short. It is interesting in this context to make a comparison with previous enlargements of the EU. For the first two central European countries that applied for membership (Hungary and Poland) the accession negotiations lasted for four years ten months, while the overall process (from application to accession) took ten years one month. For the other countries the periods were correspondingly less. For the enlargement of 1995, the duration was shorter: only one year one month for the negotiations, and for the overall process two years nine months (Finland) three years six months (Sweden) and five years five months (Austria). It is hardly surprising that the progress of these EFTA countries, with a higher level of development than the EU, and already participating in the EEA, was more rapid. For the 'southern' enlargement of the EU in 1986, however, the duration was rather similar to that for the central Europeans: for the negotiations six years eight months (Portugal) and six years four months (Spain), for the overall process eight years nine months (Portugal) and eight years five months (Spain).

Such comparisons can naturally be qualified by other arguments. For example, the central European countries would surely consider their accession process as starting with the events of 1989–90, or at Copenhagen in 1993. But these figures show that the enlargement process for the countries joining in 2004 was broadly in line with what could be predicted from past experience.

Results of the negotiations

The question whether the results of the accession negotiations were satisfactory can be answered in the first place by the fact that they were accepted by the negotiators and ratified by their constituents. In the case of the EU, they were approved by its institutions and member states, and in the case of the applicant countries by their parliaments and by national referendums in all ten countries except Cyprus.

The results of the negotiations surely fulfilled most of the expectations of the applicant countries, at least for those who analysed the prospects realistically. In fact, the conduct of the final stages in 2002 was arguably less conflictual than some participants expected. This was partly due to the effectiveness of the road-map in clearing the way for the end-game, but also to the fact that a number of difficult issues, not directly related to the *acquis*, were kept out of the negotiations: for example, in the case of the Czech Republic the 'Beneš decrees', contested in German circles, and the nuclear power plant at Temelin, unpopular in Austria.

Rather long transitional periods were obtained by the applicant countries in areas where the *acquis* presented economic or political problems, including a number of cases of sensitivity to consumers or other sectors of society. The overall EU budgetary package, giving the assurance of no reduction in receipts and indeed the prospect of increased receipts for the new members, supported the logic of accession. But the results of the negotiations plainly did not fulfil all their hopes. The long transitional periods on which the EU insisted for free movement of workers and for the introduction of agricultural payments were difficult for them to digest and were perceived by public opinion as a kind of 'second-class membership'.

However, the high levels of support for EU membership registered in most of the referendums in the acceding countries show that such disappointments in the negotiations did not undermine popular support for accession. In fact, the aspect of the referendums which most often attracted comment was not the result but the rate of participation.

Will the results of the negotiations have longer-term consequences for the attitudes of the acceding countries within the EU? As members, they will be shaping the *acquis*, not just accepting it. Their behaviour will certainly be influenced by the experience of the budgetary negotiations: not only in the field of agriculture, where their agricultural interests will wish to obtain equal conditions with other members as rapidly as possible but in regional policy where the demand for comparable treatment will be similar. These questions will surely be revisited in the EU's negotiations on the post-2006 budgetary framework, when the new members will be in a better negotiating position than they were as applicants. They will no doubt also press for the restrictions on free movement of workers to be lifted by other member states.

Conclusion

The enlargement negotiations of 1998–2003 were the culmination of a historic process that brought the countries of central and eastern Europe back fully into the European political and economic sphere. Although they waited for more than a decade for membership of the EU, the time was needed for adequate preparation and the prospect of membership was instrumental in helping them to pursue reforms. The negotiations themselves, despite some frustration on the part of the applicant countries, were conducted without major setback, and concluded on time. As the EU's expansion continues, the process will not become easier, and, in retrospect, the preparation of the enlargement of 2004 will surely be seen as a considerable success.

References

Avery, G. and Cameron, F. (1998) *The Enlargement of the European Union*, Sheffield: Sheffield Academic Press.

Further reading

Avery, G. (2002) 'Endgame for EU Enlargement', *Prospect* 76 (July).

Grabbe, H. (2001) *Profiting from EU Enlargement*, London: Centre for European Reform.

Kok, W. (2003) *Enlarging the European Union: Achievements and Challenges*, Florence: European University Institute.

Mayhew, A. (1998) *Recreating Europe*, Cambridge: Cambridge University Press.

Mayhew, A. (December 2000) *Enlargement of the European Union: An Analysis of the Negotiations with the Central and East European Countries*, S.E.I. Working Paper no. 39, Brighton: Sussex European Institute.

Mayhew, A. (April 2002) *The Negotiating Position of the European Union on Agriculture, the Structural Funds and the EU Budget*, S.E.I. Working Paper no. 52, Brighton: Sussex European Institute.

Mayhew, A. (May 2003) *The Financial and Budgetary Impact of Enlargement and Accession*, S.E.I. Working Paper no. 65, Brighton: Sussex European Institute.

http://europa.eu.int/comm/enlargement/

4   The newcomers

Heather Grabbe

Summary

This chapter is about what the new members will bring into the EU. Until the end of negotiations, the new members were reluctant to stake out their positions in EU debates. When they join in May 2004, however, their views will affect the balance of opinion in the Union on many critical issues. Their domestic debates have been developing since the negotiations finished, as the referendum campaigns have raised public awareness of the EU and what membership will mean. At the same time, the 'future of Europe' debate conducted through the European Convention in 2002–3 inspired journalists, think-tanks and parliamentarians in the region to examine their countries' interests in more detail. The Convention involved the candidate countries fully in EU business for the first time.

Introduction

In the existing EU-15, the debate about the impact of enlargement has so far concentrated on two big issues: the effects on the budget and the EU's institutions. The Union's membership will grow by two-thirds, which will have a massive effect on its institutional functioning, and the new members are considerably poorer on average than the current member states. The budget question has been resolved for the moment, with a fairly small amount of money allocated to the new members, although the financing issue will re-emerge in the years ahead, as this chapter will discuss. The institutional questions have been partially addressed by the Convention, although this issue is also likely to come back quite soon after enlargement.

There will also be qualitative changes as the new members add their own priorities to the EU's agenda. The political balance will change as the new members weigh in on one side of the argument or the other on most issues. The impact of enlargement on the EU's internal alliances and debates has been little considered in either present or future member states, so this chapter sketches out how the newcomers will change the political scene (see Appendix for a list of the new members).

Among commentators, officials and politicians there are three prevalent assumptions about the future behaviour of the new members. The first is that the new members will vote as a bloc in the EU's decision-making. The second is that they will be meek policy-takers which will follow the lead of Germany and other large member states. Finally, some commentators assume that they will join the federalist camp along with the small Benelux members of the Union. All three of these assumptions are likely to be false, as this chapter will demonstrate.

Historical legacies and expectations of the return to Europe

The ten countries that applied to join the EU are extremely diverse in their histories and current circumstances. Six of them are newly independent: the three Baltic states (Estonia, Latvia and Lithuania), the Czech Republic and Slovakia (formerly Czechoslovakia) and Slovenia (formerly part of Yugoslavia). Having just regained sovereignty, they tend to dislike terms like 'federation' (as in Yugoslav) and 'Union' (as in Soviet). What is appealing about the European Union is the voluntary nature of membership and the right of every member to have a say in its decision-making.

All of the central European countries have been part of a wider empire at some point in their history, Hapsburg, Ottoman, Russian or Soviet. This makes them very keen to keep their hard-won independence. Most people see independence as best defended by integration into the wider region, hence the enthusiasm with which they have already integrated politically and economically with the EU. They are acutely conscious of their own vulnerable geographic position between West and East.

All the countries have wanted to join every available international club, from the OSCE, OECD and WTO, to NATO and the EU. After half a century of communism, the political class was very keen to become a 'normal' country again, and being normal meant being fully part of the European mainstream. For the central and east Europeans, membership of the EU and NATO was a fast-track into that mainstream.

Another historical factor is an enormous sensitivity in central Europe to minority issues and the legacy of the Second World War. Many minorities live side by side in central Europe and nationalism remains an explosive political force. For example, 2002 saw a number of election campaigns across central Europe which featured the issue of the expulsion of ethnic Germans from neighbouring countries that took place after 1945. Despite the formal reconciliation between governments and the official settlement of most compensation claims, issues like the post-war Beneš decrees were still alive in political campaigning more than fifty years later. The Cold War effectively 'froze' many of these issues and sentiments in the region run high.

Identity is another vital issue, and one that affects how people see the EU. Politicians like former Estonian Prime Minister, Mart Laar, see the

Union as a great defender of minority culture, and membership as a way of guaranteeing that no small nation is ever forced to learn a larger neighbour's language as his countrymen did in the Soviet era. Others claim the EU is dangerous for national identity. Czech President, Vaclav Klaus, has repeatedly warned that the Czechs must not allow their identity to be dissolved in the EU 'like a lump of sugar in a cup of coffee'. These concerns about identity lie behind the widespread wariness about any EU policies that might threaten the unity of states, such as autonomy for regions with sizeable minorities.

Size is one of the reasons behind these sensitivities. Apart from Poland, the ten newcomers joining in 2004 are small and they will be concerned to defend their position *vis-à-vis* the bigger countries, just as current members like the Benelux countries, Denmark, Ireland and Sweden have done. Central European political debates are still developing, but they show signs of becoming assertive in defending what they see as vital interests. The nine small countries will want to ensure that the Union is not run primarily by the 'big boys'.

The new members are also used to competition. In the past decade, they have principally competed against one another, for foreign direct investment, for trade and to be ready for EU membership and not fall behind their neighbours in the negotiations. This regional competition has helped their economies to be competitive in the single market and in global markets. But it comes at the cost of regional co-operation. Many regional and sub-regional initiatives were started, but bilateral relations with the EU were always more exciting politically and rewarding economically. For example, tariff barriers between members of the CEFTA did not fall as fast as the trade concessions made by the EU; and the EU refused to negotiate collectively with the four members of the Višegrad Group. This tendency to compete is likely to continue once the new members join the Union. Rather than forming an 'eastern bloc', each new member will form its own alliances with the other member states, depending on its interests.

The legacy of the negotiations

The accession negotiations have left a bitter taste in central Europe because the financial deal was not generous to the new member states. The EU-15 countries have become progressively less generous about helping their poorer neighbours as growth in the eurozone economies has slowed and national budgets have been squeezed by the need to keep within the Stability and Growth Pact rules. The member states are feeling much less generous now than they might have been if enlargement had taken place during the economic upswing of the late 1990s.

The new members are relatively poor countries, with income per head between one-third and two-thirds of the EU average. All are keen to gain more assistance from the EU's budget to help them catch up with the current members. So they will have a common interest in the budget battle once they join.

The total package of financial aid under the current budget, which runs until the end of 2006, amounts to a maximum of 40.8 billion euro. This sum includes money for agriculture subsidies, infrastructure spending, regional aid and funds to help improve nuclear safety, public administration and border protection. However, the new members will also pay contributions to the EU budget, amounting to some 15 billion euro during 2004–6. Moreover, they may not be able to use all the money that has been allocated to them in the budget by 2006. As a result, the net cost of enlargement could be just 10.3 billion euro for ten countries over three years, according to Commission figures (see Grabbe 2002). That is a minuscule amount of money, less than one-thousandth of EU gross domestic product. Even the gross amount is below the ceiling agreed for enlargement at the Berlin European Council in 1999 of just over 42 billion euro. Moreover, the money for the new members is ring-fenced from the rest of the budget, so enlargement cannot become an unlimited financial liability.

Budget battle ahead

The EU's budget is one area of the Union where the new members already have clear interests and an active domestic debate. It is also the one area where the new members have a common interest, because they are all considerably poorer than the EU average. The main splits in this debate will be between the net contributors to the budget, the old net recipients (Spain, Portugal and Greece) and the new net recipients.

However, even on this issue, there is a difference between the interests of the richest and poorest of the new members. For example, compare Slovenia, which is already richer than Greece and Portugal and will probably become a net contributor soon after accession, with Latvia, which has a GDP per capita of less than half Slovenia's level. Although these two countries will both want the EU to continue funding economic convergence, they will have different interests in what kinds of policies are funded by the EU budget.

The new members will fight hard for more money in the next financial period, likely to run from 2007–13, to gain back some of what they lost in the accession negotiations. The debate about the budget will start in 2004–5. Previously, the candidates were perceived as competing for funds with the poorer countries among the existing member states: Polish farmers have been pitted against Spanish and French recipients. After accession, however, Poland could become Spain's friend, teaming up to demand a budget that goes above the current ceiling of 1.27 per cent of EU GDP.

The big question is whether the new members will want to change the structure of the budget. Until the final period of the negotiations, most of the candidates seemed likely to favour a more logical budget, targeting help to the poorest parts of the enlarged Union. Many of their policy-makers regarded it absurd that the EU spends nearly half of its budget on agriculture, and a tiny proportion on economic reform.

However, after they join, the new members' stances in the fiscal debate could be based mainly on getting their hands on more money within the status quo, not changing the rules completely, because their farmers will start receiving money from Brussels that they will be unwilling to give up. The structure of the accession deal means that the largest transfers from Brussels go to the new members in the form of cheques to farmers. The EU has thus created political constituencies in central Europe which have an interest in maintaining transfers under the CAP. This will make it more difficult for the enlarged Union to reform the budget as a whole away from agricultural subsidies.

The new members have lobbies of farming interests that could turn their governments against radical agricultural reforms. The 'mid-term review' of interim reforms to start before 2007 is supposed to cut the link between subsidies and production still further and divert more funds from direct payments to farmers into funds for rural development. These reforms would make the CAP more suitable for central European agriculture, which suffers from under-development and a need for modernisation. But once central European farmers, especially in Poland, where they are most numerous, start to receive cheques from Brussels in 2004, they will lobby their governments to continue the system of direct payments. Although farming lobbies in the region may decline in strength as they age and people leave the land, they are likely to be powerful in the critical years for deciding the next financial perspective.

However, even if the new members focus first on funds for agriculture, owing to the legacy of the negotiations they are likely to benefit most from the structural and cohesion funds in the longer term. The EU's regional aid is supposed to encourage economic convergence across the EU. As the poorest members of the enlarged EU, and hence needing most help with convergence, the central and east Europeans can expect to be the major beneficiaries from these funds.

The EU's regional aid policies will have to be overhauled to take account of the additional economic and social disparities that the new members will bring into the Union. A major question about the future of regional aid is whether or not it becomes focused primarily on the new members, with little or no money going to the richer member states, as the UK Treasury proposed in March 2003 (HM Treasury). At first sight, such a refocusing would suit the new members, because their needs would take priority in allocation of the funds. But the richest old members, and especially Germany, which makes the largest net contribution to the EU budget, would then have no reason to allocate large sums to the structural and cohesion funds. None of their regions would have a stake in the struc-tural funds, so the richest countries would have no incentive to allocate much money to that part of the budget. Thus some of the new members might decide it is in their long-term interest to team up with the poorer regions in the richer countries, such as the eastern Länder of Germany, to argue that regional aid should go to the poorest parts of every member state, rather than renationalising regional policy.

The new members' positions in the budget battle will also be affected by the costs of accession. Their finance ministers are likely to need more transfers from Brussels because several of them will face considerable problems with public finances in the first years of EU membership. National budgets will take a 'triple whammy' when the new members join the EU.

EU-related spending will increase as they implement the more expensive parts of the EU's rules and regulations, in order to meet the promises they have made in negotiations. This could add between 5 and 15 per cent to EU-related expenditure in Poland, for example. The new members' finance ministries will have to find more money to co-finance infrastructure projects, in order to qualify for EU budgetary transfers. Several have promised to give extra payments to farmers on top of the 25 per cent from the EU. In Poland's case, this could be one billion euro, amounting to some 3 per cent of the total national budget. At the same time, the new members will be trying to qualify for monetary union, so they have to trim their budget deficits down to 3 per cent of GDP. That will be very hard, given all the additional expenditure, if growth rates do not increase dramatically.

The likely outcome is a fiscal squeeze in the first few years of accession, which could result in higher levels of public borrowing. Over the medium term, all of the new member states are likely to undertake structural reform of public finances, partly as a result of these pressures from the European Union.

The EU has tried to ease the burden by providing the new members with a cash flow facility, which for Poland will amount to nearly one billion euro for 2004, plus 650 million euro in 2005 and 550 million euro in 2006. In addition, they will all get temporary budgetary compensation to ensure that no new member becomes a net contributor. The EU's decision to set 1 May 2004 as the date of accession, rather than 1 January 2004, also helps because the new members will get a full year's worth of receipts from the 2004 budget, but will make monthly contributions for only eight months of the year.

However, several candidates whose budget deficits are already rising, most notably the Czech Republic, Hungary and Poland, could face a fiscal crunch that will make their governments unpopular. The EU could also become unpopular, if it is blamed for the budget problems. In 2004, the new members will not get substantially more money from Brussels than they did as candidates in 2003. At the same time, they will have to spend more on the things that the EU wants, like environmental standards and infrastructure, so there will be less money available for popular items like education, healthcare and pensions. Moreover, the EU-related spending will cause the level of fixed expenditure in the national budgets to rise, with less discretionary spending available if public finances run into trouble owing to other problems, for example floods or higher unemployment. The political effect could be that the EU gets the blame for the fiscal problems, making it unpopular among voters.

Like Britain, Spain and Portugal before them, the central and eastern European countries might spend their first years of membership trying to renegotiate what they saw as unfair accession terms. The new member states could also be driven by their domestic politics to take an obstructive stance in the negotiations about the EU's next budget plan, which will run from 2007 onwards. That would weaken the sense of solidarity between member states on which the budget is supposed to be based. It would also make the enlarged EU acrimonious, rather than welcoming. The greatest political risk is that the new members will focus their time and energy after accession on fighting for additional euros from the budget, rather than helping the Union to reform itself, function better and agree new policies.

The referendum campaigns and the question of 'Europe' in party politics

One of the central determinants of how a member state behaves in the EU is the state of its domestic debate about Europe. Countries that have a strong consensus in favour of European integration, like Ireland and Finland, tend to have a more consistent approach to the EU that gives them more influence over time than countries where opinion is divided, like the UK and Denmark. The debates about the EU developing in the new member states are very diverse in their scope and content, suggesting that these countries will behave differently once they join.

Until the final phase of the accession negotiations, discussion of European integration was confined to a small political elite. Only the negotiating team, the EU liaison departments and some ministers were involved in European matters at a detailed level. Much of the political class still knew very little about the EU's policies and how it was organised, while the public had a fairly hazy notion of what EU membership involved. That situation began to change in 2003, once the negotiations were over and governments began campaigns to persuade their countrymen of the merits of joining the EU.

All of the new members but Cyprus held a referendum on EU membership in the course of 2003. They resulted in higher levels of support for accession than opinion polls, and many politicians, had expected. A positive result was most uncertain in Malta, where public opinion was almost evenly divided on whether to join, and the Labour Party (the main opposition party, which usually gets about half the vote) campaigned strongly against membership. In the end, Maltese accession scraped through, with nearly 54 per cent in favour and a very high turnout of 91 per cent. Poland's referendum was also a nail-biter, because the turnout had to reach 50 per cent for the result to be valid. In the event, both the turnout and the 'yes' vote were strong. Table 4.1 shows the outcome of all the referenda.

Strong euroscepticism is still confined to fringe parties in most central European countries. Only in Malta and the Czech Republic do one of the main parties express strong doubts about the principle of EU membership. Czech President Vaclav Klaus is the only major political figure in central Europe to attack the EU consistently, and even he did not explicitly tell Czechs to vote 'no' in the referendum. He was the only president, however, who did not strongly support his country's EU membership.

The fringe parties which attacked the EU in the referendum campaign have had some success in frightening the most vulnerable sections of the population, the poor, elderly and rural voters. The EU will be an obvious target after accession too, as few of the benefits of membership will be obvious to the population immediately. The new members have already experienced most of the economic benefits thanks to integration over the past decade and the political benefits will emerge over the longer term. It could also take some time for the cash from Brussels to start flowing. Some new members are unlikely to absorb all the funds that are available because their public administrations are not fully ready for the CAP and regional aid.

However, the costs of accession will become more visible. The Commission is clamping down on enforcement of the EU's rules and regulations, using the threat of the 'safeguard clauses' negotiated at Copenhagen. At the same time, a fiscal squeeze on national budgets could result from the costs of accession, co-financing and attempts to qualify for the euro. These developments will provide a ready target for eurosceptic politicians.

In many countries, the right has been seeking a new way of defining itself in the past few years, as anti-communism has waned as an electoral

Table 4.1 Referenda in accession countries

Country	Whether binding	Date in 2003	Result %	Turnout %
Malta	Not binding	8 March	54 yes, 46 no	91
Slovenia	Not binding	23 March	90 yes, 10 no	60
Hungary	Binding	12 April	84 yes, 16 no	46
Lithuania	Binding	10–11 May	91 yes, 9 no	63
Slovakia	Binding	16–17 May	92 yes, 6 no	52
Poland	Binding	7–8 June	77 yes, 23 no	59
Czech Republic	Binding	13–14 June	77 yes, 23 no	55
Estonia	Binding	14 September	67 yes, 33 no	64
Latvia	Binding	20 September	67 yes, 32 no	73
Cyprus	No referendum	–	–	–

issue. So it is likely to use this opportunity for anti-EU campaigns to distinguish itself from left-wing parties. By coincidence, the left is in power in many of the new member states, Czech Republic, Hungary, Lithuania, Poland, Slovenia, just when they are joining. As left-wing governments negotiated many of the deals at Copenhagen, it would be easy for the right to criticise their position on Europe in election campaigns in the first years after membership.

Trends in public opinion

So far, the public debates about European integration in the candidate countries have focused on the question of joining the EU, when it might happen and whether other countries might join first. There has not been detailed debate about different aspects of the EU and how it works.

Public opinion on joining the EU has been fairly consistent since the late 1990s. The general trend has been for support for EU membership to decline as countries come closer to joining the EU. The Union becomes less of an abstract ideal and more of a reality as membership approaches. The highest levels of support are among the countries that will not join in 2004, Bulgaria, Romania and Turkey. The other countries show levels of support ranging between one-third and two-thirds of the population. The Baltic states and Malta have long had the lowest levels of support and Estonia, Latvia and Malta also have the highest levels of open opposition to membership, between a fifth and nearly a quarter of the population. In all of the countries, opinion poll surveys reveal a large proportion of 'don't knows' among respondents. (*Eurobarometer* does regular surveys of support for the EU in accession countries. See: http://europa.eu.int/comm/public_opinion/enlargement_en.htm)

Among the 2004 entrants, Hungary has long had one of the highest levels of EU support, followed by Slovakia and Cyprus. During the early and mid-1990s Poland had very high levels of support – above 70 per cent – which fell to just above 50 per cent when the negotiations about financial transfers began. The referendum campaigns raised the level of support well above the majority required – but support may fall again once accession is achieved.

Once the new members join the EU, public opinion is likely to change, because people's views will be formed by what they see of the Union. One of the first issues on which they will start to form views is the EU's new constitutional treaty. Several of the new members' governments are considering holding referenda on the constitutional treaty after it is finalised by the IGC. For some countries, this referendum could be both a replay of the one on membership, and also a poll on the performance of the government of the day. The treaty could raise fears about the EU if it is portrayed by eurosceptic politicians and the media as a development that infringes national sovereignty. Either way, it will raise greater awareness of the EU among the public.

Emerging attitudes towards European integration

The new members experienced a crash course in the debate about European integration through the Convention. For the first time, the new members were invited to take part fully in a European debate. They sent government representatives and parliamentarians and their NGOs and policy institutes were actively involved in the debate surrounding the Convention's deliberations. This inclusion was welcome, but it was also rather odd, since institutional reform is an abstract issue on which the candidate countries had the least well-developed views, since they had not yet been involved in EU decision-making.

In the first nine months of the Convention's work, representatives from the candidate countries were unwilling to take firm policy positions on European integration. Many reasoned: 'Why antagonise one or other group of member states while we are still negotiating entry?' Moreover, they did not have strong views on the method of European integration or the precise configuration of the EU's institutions, since their politicians and officials had not worked within it. Their main interlocutor during the accession negotiations was the European Commission but they were less acquainted with the Council of Ministers, the European Parliament or the European Court of Justice.

However, once the negotiations were over, the representatives from the new members began to be more active in the Convention. Two who made an important impact were Alojz Peterle, the Slovenian parliamentarian, who was the candidates' representative on the Convention's Presidium, and Danuta Hübner, the representative of the Polish government, the only large country about to join the Union.

The new members identified with the smaller member states on many issues. For example, all except Poland signed a letter organised by the small countries during the Convention, objecting to the creation of a permanent president of the European Council. But judging by their behaviour in the Convention, the new members are unlikely to be as federalist as the Benelux countries. The political elites in central Europe are not ideologically committed to the traditional 'community method' of decision-making. Rather, they tend to consider pragmatically what is the best way of developing a policy. For example, they are generally in favour of the 'Lisbon process' for economic reform, which does not work through the EU's institutions in the traditional way, but through a process of benchmarking and peer pressure (Murray 2003).

Policy-makers in central Europe have changed their views on the Commission. The new members saw the Commission's hard face during the negotiations, when it was the body on the other side of the table making demands and telling them what to do. However, even though the high-handed attitude of some Commission representatives caused annoyance, the members-to-be came to see its utility as guardian of the treaties and a defender of the small countries. In the final phase of negotiations, the Commission fought hard to defend the timetable for enlargement. It was seen to be 'tough but fair', in the words of one Polish diplomat. During the Convention, most of the central European representatives supported a greater role for the Commission in enforcing a level playing field for the single market. For example, their countries suffered from Commission criticism of inward investment incentives and state aids, most of which they were obliged to abolish before joining the EU. Many new members, however, now see that it is in their interest for the Commission to enforce such rules strictly. Otherwise, the richer, old member states could afford to offer bigger incentives and aid to companies, thereby distorting competition and placing the poorer members at a disadvantage.

The new member representatives in the Convention were generally opposed to moves that would allow the large countries to dominate EU decision-making on foreign policy and defence. They are wary of inter-governmentalism in areas where it would diminish their status. All of the new members want to have a Commissioner who has voting rights. However, there is a contradiction between their wish to have a strong, effective Commission and their desire for full Commissioners from every member-state, which will weaken the Commission by making it less cohesive.

The new members are still struggling to define their interests in many of the EU's policy areas. They were not allowed to join either the EU's single currency or the Schengen area of passport-free travel immediately on accession, although the new members are also not allowed a formal opt-out from parts of the EU, like the UK and Denmark. As a result, two of the most pressing policy issues after achieving membership will be to work towards fulfilling the criteria for the euro and Schengen. Both will be very challenging because the euro entry criteria are onerous for fast-growing economies (Barysch and Grabbe 2002); and meeting the Schengen requirements will require them to introduce more expensive and controversial border controls with neighbouring countries that remain outside the EU. In both cases, the new members' goal in EU policy debates will be to ensure that the entry criteria for these policy areas do not become stricter and to ask for assistance to help them comply. Other areas where the new members are likely to be active are environmental and social regulations. Businesses operating in central and eastern Europe have already had to meet high EU standards for producing goods for sale in the single market. If richer, old member states propose higher process standards for industry, the new members are likely to object because such standards whittle away their comparative advantage by driving up production costs and deterring foreign direct investment. At the least, the new members are likely to demand EU financial assistance to help them meet any new regulations that will be expensive for the public sector to implement.

Views on foreign policy

The newcomers' foreign policies are mostly focused on their neighbours, not the wider world. Their main external policy priorities in the past 15 years have been accession to the EU and NATO and bilateral relations. Like the smaller, present member states, they may choose to interest themselves in just a few issues in foreign policy, rather than taking a global view. Some of the new members could become rather ambivalent about further enlargement of the EU. So far, they have publicly supported Bulgarian and Romanian ambitions to join, but they are more divided about Turkey, as are the present member states. Polish Prime Minister, Leszek Miller, and former Czech President, Vaclav Havel, have argued in favour of Turkey joining, but others are opposed. The key issue is whether the integration of further countries will divert EU funds away from them and diminish their status.

How active will the new members be in EU external policy-making? In particular, will Poland develop a large country mentality or a small country mentality in this field? By virtue of its population, although not its economy, Poland will be one of the big six member states. It might be expected to take a major role in foreign policy, as France and Britain do, given its size and military tradition. Poland has been to the fore in advocating the development of a stronger EU foreign policy. Early in 2003, the Polish foreign ministry published a regional strategy for the EU to deal with the countries to its east. But even that policy paper was more about the country's immediate neighbours than about Russia.

All of the new members have complex views about Russia and the EU's future relationship with it. They had different relationships with the Soviet Union during half a century of communism, but there is little nostalgia for a closer relationship with Russia. People over the age of 40 have first-hand memories of political and cultural oppression and economic dependence. Stalin's attempts to wipe out central European political elites after the Second World War are not forgotten. Some countries suffered invasions, and the three Baltic states were annexed by the Soviet Union. Such experiences cause instinctive suspicions about Russian motivations in forging a closer relationship with the EU. The legacies of the twentieth century live on, not just in people's memories but in practical issues. For example, the EU made fair treatment of the large Russian-speaking minorities in Estonia and Latvia part of the accession criteria for those countries. It also negotiated transit arrangements and a visa regime with Russia for the people living in the Russian enclave of Kaliningrad, sandwiched between Poland, Lithuania and the Baltic Sea. Both issues arose as a result of Soviet policy in the region during and after the Second World War. However, some politicians in the region are beginning to see the virtues of the EU developing a more substantive relationship with Russia, the Caucasus and other parts of the former Soviet Union. It may well become easier to deal with Russia, in economic and political matters, through the EU. The new members will have a full role in negotiating this relationship with Russia and it will give them a better position *vis-à-vis* Moscow than if they were negotiating bilaterally. Like the smaller members of the EU, they gain more standing in international negotiations by being part of the EU.

Attitudes towards the United States

The behaviour of the prospective members over Iraq in 2003 confirmed the prejudices of many in France that they will be pro-American. When most central and eastern European states announced their support for the enforcement of UN Security Council Resolution 1441, they seemed to vindicate Donald Rumsfeld, the US Defence Secretary, who announced in January that the EU's new members would be Washington's loyal allies, opposed to the 'old Europe' of Germany and France. Rumsfeld is right that the EU's new members are Atlanticists, preferring to work with rather than against the United States. But it would be wrong to assume that they will align themselves with Washington on every issue.

The test of loyalty over Iraq came at an awkward moment. The US Senate was considering ratification of the second enlargement of NATO. All of the central and eastern European countries chose to support the US in its attempt to gain approval for military action. The Czech Republic, Hungary and Poland signed the 'Letter of the Eight' (along with Denmark, Italy, Portugal, Spain and the UK), which was solicited and published by the *Wall Street Journal*, calling for European unity in the Security Council on enforcement of Resolution 1441. A week later, the ten candidates for NATO membership issued their own letter, one that was organised by Bruce Jackson, an American who had lobbied effectively to get them accepted by the Atlantic alliance. How could they say no?

'As the EU enlarges eastwards, its centre of gravity will move westwards,' a senior British diplomat has predicted, hoping that it will bring Europe's heart closer to London than to Paris. The new member states will certainly tip the balance towards support for NATO and away from France and other countries wanting to create a European counterweight to American power. When faced with the choice of saying yes or no to the United States, they said yes. But it was an unwelcome dilemma for countries that want a strong Europe too.

The Iraq war was a special case, however, and Washington cannot count on their support for further military adventures. The text of the two famous letters declared support for upholding UN Security Council resolutions and maintaining the credibility of international institutions. Neither letter advocated the use of force or offered the US *carte blanche* to pursue disarmament by any means it chose. Their position was more Blairite than pro-Bush, in trying to encourage the United States to work through international institutions.

Public opinion in the central and east European countries was overwhelmingly against the war, just as it was in the rest of Europe. On most foreign policy issues, the CEECs tend to side with the EU not the US. They are strongly multilateralist, having suffered greatly from superpower domination during the Cold War. Moreover, Rumsfeld's dividing line does not run through all of foreign policy. The new members want a strong transatlantic alliance, but they also want the EU to have an effective foreign policy, especially in the Balkans and the eastern fringe of the enlarged Union. It is true that they will pull the EU's centre of gravity westwards towards the Atlantic alliance but they will also pull European foreign policy eastwards, towards their potentially troublesome neighbours. In addition to Poland's proposals for developing the EU's *Ostpolitik*, Hungary and Slovenia want to integrate the Balkans politically and economically into the European mainstream. The enlarged Union's unstable periphery, to the east and south, is of diminishing importance to Washington, but it is of vital concern to the new members. They will push it up the political agenda in Brussels at every opportunity.

On most international issues, the new members are increasingly 'European' in their preferences. They support the EU on issues like non-proliferation, the Kyoto protocol, the death penalty and the ICC, despite strong US pressure. They usually vote with the other Europeans in the UN and align themselves with the EU's common positions on CFSP. Their voting patterns are not motivated by a wish to curry favour with the EU, but by their changing views on international affairs. As they move closer to membership, countries become increasingly 'socialised' in the EU's ways of doing business. Their political classes have grown to think like the EU's current members, including on international issues.

In France, there is a widely held view that the new members will be pro-American and seek to turn the EU into no more than a free trade area as the British are suspected of doing. But these countries have not made enormous efforts to join the Union in order to turn it into a free trade area. They have already had much of the economic benefits prior to accession: free trade in industrial products, foreign direct investment and a large amount of aid. What they want from membership is full participation in the political decisions being made in Europe including foreign policy, security and defence. Most people in the region do not see a contradiction between supporting NATO and advocating effective defence capabilities for the EU.

France and the idea of a 'core Europe'

Central and eastern Europe has often suffered from decisions made by great powers outside the region. Politicians in the region know that, to be able to choose freely, you have to be on equal terms with your partners. They can only have equality if they are fully involved in the EU's decision-making. The new members fear that important decisions will be taken by a group of big countries and imposed upon the rest. They dread a *directoire* of big countries, bullying the others into submission.

For this reason, the new members are wary of the ambitions of some French, German and Belgian politicians to create a 'core Europe'. They do not want to gain admission to the EU only to discover that an inner sanctum has been created that excludes them. Moreover, France's leaders have already created resentment thanks to their haughty attitude towards the candidate countries. Jacques Chirac's insults to the new members during the Iraq crisis worked in the short term: central and east European leaders kept a low profile over Iraq, not wishing to jeopardise their accession in 2004. It is possible that this public scolding will cost France dearly in the longer term by alienating potential allies.

The new members' growing mistrust of France started long before the Iraq crisis. The reluctance of French leaders François Mitterrand and Edouard Balladur in the early 1990s to agree to eastward enlargement has not been forgotten. Then at the Nice summit in 2000, which decided the number of votes in the Council and seats in the European Parliament to be allocated to the new members, Chirac said that old member states, who contributed to the Union from its foundation, should have more votes that those who are new and will bring problems (*Economist*, 16 December 2000). Just after the 1989 revolutions, there was widespread Francophilia in central and eastern Europe, thanks to the dissidents who had spent time in Paris and to the French-speaking intellectuals in Warsaw, Prague, Bucharest and Sofia. That cultural admiration has been tainted by mistrust and anger at the attitude of France's politicians towards enlargement.

Conclusion

The new members are unlikely to be interested in all the areas of EU activity. They are finding it difficult to define their interests in many EU policies and they are still at a formative stage of finding their positions. It will take a few years before the new members are fully engaged in every part of EU business. A few issues unite them. They are all likely to favour financial transfers to poor regions, for example, but they have different views on many others. The unifying factor of being candidates will dissolve after accession. Other splits in the EU, for example, between big and small, Atlanticist and European on security, are likely to become much more important than old versus new members.

The new members will all favour a larger budget for the EU, with funds concentrated on the poor areas of the Union, most of which will lie in central and eastern Europe. But on issues like economic policy and defence they are unlikely to vote as a bloc. Estonia has perhaps the most liberal economy in Europe, whereas Polish instincts are often more protectionist. Poland is a strong Atlanticist when it comes to defence. But most other central Europeans see no potential conflict between supporting NATO and building ESDP. A small rural country like Lithuania does not necessarily have the same objectives as wealthier, central European countries, such as the Czech Republic and Slovenia, with their diversified, export-oriented industries. Poland, with 40 million people, will behave differently in the EU from Latvia with its 2.5 million population.

Three prevalent assumptions about the future behaviour of the new members are wrong. They are unlikely to form a bloc on most issues. Rather than acting in unison, they will team up with the existing member states, depending on the issues at hand. Enlargement could thus change the debate in areas such as tax harmonisation or defence policy. For example, Poland will join the UK in opposing tax harmonisation and supporting NATO, but it could be a friend of Spain in wanting to increase the size of the EU budget.

The new members are unlikely to be meek policy-takers and will bring in new ideas and priorities. The budget debate will be the first big test of how assertive they will be as member states. The new members have a decade of experience of economic reform and democratisation, so they could become impatient with the EU's slow progress in structural reform. Several of them have active relationships with the new neighbours of the Union, which will be an asset in EU foreign policy. Poland's engagement with Ukraine will make Warsaw a strong advocate of a more active eastern policy for the Union, while Hungary will contribute to the EU's thinking on its southern neighbours in the Balkans. In foreign policy, New/Old Europe is not a division that will last long. Iraq was a special case. The new members are instinctively Atlanticist while also generally supporting the development of European foreign and security policies. But can they put up enough money to pull their weight in new defence initiatives?

Finally, the new members are unlikely to be as federalist as the Benelux countries. The Convention debates showed that most of them are concerned to ensure that the large member states do not dominate the Union. However, politicians in the region are less sure about whether the community method should be applied in all policy areas, for example, foreign policy. The new members will upset many of the long-standing political alliances in the Union on issues ranging from foreign policy to agriculture.

Overall, this enlargement is likely to lead to a further deepening of European integration. As Fraser Cameron argues in Chapter 1, every previous widening has led to significantly more integration, from the evolution of regional policy and the single market after Greece, Portugal and Spain joined in the 1980s, to the expansion of the Schengen area and the launch of the euro after Austria, Finland and Sweden entered in 1995. The challenges faced by the newcomers of 2004 will require the EU to develop new policies, particularly to deal with economic disparities, border controls and relations with the EU's new neighbours. There will thus not necessarily be a trade-off between deepening and widening. However, the

EU will need to find new methods of allowing integration to continue as it grows increasingly diverse.

References

Barysch, K. and Grabbe, H. (2002) *Who's Ready for EU Enlargement,* London: Centre for European Reform.

Grabbe, H. (2002) 'The Copenhagen deal for enlargement', CER briefing note, London: Centre for European Reform, December.

HM Treasury, Department of Trade and Industry and the Office of the Deputy Prime Minister (2003) *A Modern Regional Policy for the United Kingdom,* London: The Stationery Office.

Murray, A. (2003) *The Lisbon Scorecard III: The Status of Economic Reform in the Enlarging EU,* London: Centre for European Reform.

Further reading

Boeri, T. *et al.* (2002) *Who's Afraid of the Big Enlargement? Economic and Social Implications of the European Union's Prospective Eastward Expansion,* CEPR Policy Paper No. 7, London: Centre for Economic Policy Research.

Economist Intelligence Unit (2003) *Europe Enlarged: Understanding the Impact,* London: EIU.

Grabbe, H. (2001) *Profiting from EU Enlargement,* London: Centre for European Reform.

Grabbe, H. (2002) 'EU conditionality and the *acquis communautaire',* *International Political Science Review* 23 (July 2002), 249–68.

Grabbe, H. and Hughes, K. (1998) *Enlarging the EU Eastwards,* London: RIIA/ Cassell.

Mayhew, A. (1998) *Recreating Europe: The European Union's Policy towards Central and Eastern Europe,* Cambridge: Cambridge University Press.

Sedelmeier, U. and Wallace, H. (2000) 'Eastern enlargement – strategy or second thoughts?' in H. Wallace and W. Wallace (eds) *Policy-Making in the European Union,* fourth edition, Oxford: Oxford University Press.

Taggart, P. and Szczerbiak, A. (2001) *The Party Politics of Euroscepticism: EU Member and Candidate States,* SEI Working Paper No. 51, Brighton: Sussex European Institute.

Database of research on enlargement: www.wiiw.at/countdown.

Positions in the Convention: www.epin.org and www.europa.eu.int/futurum.

Politics and economics of enlargement: www.cer.org.uk/enlargement.

5 The political economy of enlargement

Andrew Scott

Summary

The fifth enlargement of the EU involves the accession of ten new member states, eight of which are central and east European countries (CEECs). This chapter considers the economic dimension of this enlargement, particularly from the perspective of this group of eight countries. While the accession of Cyprus and Malta raises important political and institutional questions, in economic terms the countries are relatively small and pose no significant difficulties with regard to the adoption of the EU *acquis*. The chapter then reviews the pre-accession strategy before considering the broad economic realities in the accession countries. It covers the microeconomic policy and the macroeconomic dimensions of enlargement respectively.

Introduction

The fifth enlargement of the EU represents the largest geographic expansion on the part of the EU and by far the most challenging in economic terms. The eight CEECs that will join the EU in May 2004 are much poorer than the existing EU average and present a number of economic weaknesses. The nature of the attendant economic challenges are reasonably well documented and in this chapter we will elaborate on the key problems which can be expected to arise following enlargement, and consider how these might be addressed. Notwithstanding the challenges, enlargement cannot be regarded as involving only problems. The expansion of the EU internal market by up to 75 million new consumers is likely to generate economic benefits through orthodox static and dynamic trade and competition effects, which we review below. At the same time, we can reasonably expect the force of the EU in the world economy and in the multilateral agencies of international economic diplomacy and policy-making to be enhanced, as the larger EU begins to reap the benefits of being a larger and economically strengthened 'global region'.

Although enlargement will set the EU new economic and political challenges, there is no reason to expect that it will give rise to significant trade effects or adjustment problems. Indeed, in economic terms it is likely that, from the perspective of the present member states, little will change as a result of enlargement. After all, the acceding countries together have an economic weight equivalent to only 4 or 5 per cent of the gross domestic product (GDP) of the EU-15 and the period since 1993 has seen the EU progressively lowering its economic barriers to the effective economic integration of the accession countries in preparation for enlargement. Accordingly, the remaining problems concern not the formalisation of this economic integration process, but rather the adoption by the CEECs of the policies of the EU-15, referred to as the *acquis*. Despite the successful conclusion of the enlargement negotiations at Copenhagen in December 2002 and the reasonably generous transition arrangements agreed, there are still widespread concerns within the EU that the CEECs are some distance from being in a position to fulfil all the obligations of EU membership.

The pre-accession strategy

The enlargement of the EU owes much to the sometimes difficult economic reforms that were implemented within the accession states themselves. At the same time, these internal reforms were buttressed by what has come to be called the EU pre-accession, and later, the 'enhanced' pre-accession, strategy, which evolved progressively through the 1990s. The pre-accession strategy, launched at the Essen European Council in December 1994, comprised three elements:

- the PHARE programme, which dated from 1989 and which provided financial support to assist economic reforms and reconstructions in the CEECs;
- the Europe agreements, which provided for close political and economic relations as well as the asymmetric liberalisation of trade flows between the CEECs and the EU;
- a structured dialogue between the EU and the CEECs, which involved meetings between high-ranking representatives of the EU and the CEECs with a view to easing the transition to membership by including the CEECs in discussions concerning the development of particular areas of EU policy.

At the Luxembourg European Council in December 1997, the EU launched an 'enhanced pre-accession strategy' with the candidates for membership, which comprised three elements:

- accession partnerships, in the form of bilateral agreements between the EU-15 and individual candidate countries, which set out short- and medium-term priorities for action in each candidate country in preparation for membership, and which covered, *inter alia*, macro-economic stability, assimilation of EC law, progress towards meeting specific aspects of the *acquis* and outlined the ways in which the PHARE programme would support accession preparations;

- increased pre-accession financial assistance 2000–6 under the PHARE programme and the introduction of two further financial support programmes covering:

  - environmental and transport investment
  - agricultural and rural development;

- publication of regular 'progress reports' which indicate how each candidate country is proceeding in their preparations for EU membership.

Economic transition in the accession countries

The process of preparing for membership of the EU has been a difficult one for all the CEECs. Although this process only began in 1993, after the European Council meeting in Copenhagen, in effect whole-scale economic reforms had been on going in all CEECs since 1989. These reforms were designed to restructure fundamentally the economy and economic policies away from the central planning systems that had been imposed upon them by the post-1945 Soviet regime and towards market-oriented economies, in which the allocation of resources (production and consumption) was determined by a de-regulated price system underpinned by a regime of competition and private ownership. Beyond that, economic reforms also addressed the state of public finances. In all, economic reforms involved action on six fronts: macroeconomic stabilisation; price liberalisation; trade liberalisation; enterprise privatisation; the creation of a social safety net; and the emergence of an institutional structure and legal basis necessary for a market economy to function (Fisher *et al.* 1996). Indisputably these reforms were essential if the CEECs were to integrate their economies into the EU, and the global, economic system. In turn, this would trigger the process of sustained economic growth in the CEECs and provide the means of their catching up (in GDP terms) with their western European counterparts.

The conventional wisdom at the time was that the speedier this reform process, the more rapidly the transition process would be completed. In the event, however, the onset of the reform process was accompanied initially by a deep recession in each of the transition economies. Between 1989 and 1994 real output in the CEECs (excluding the former Soviet Union) fell by almost one-third, while the average rate of inflation peaked at over 60 per cent in that period. The precise causes of the recessions in the CEECs remains a matter of dispute, although most debates revolve around questions concerning the sequencing and timing of the reforms that were implemented. At one end of the spectrum was a policy of 'shock therapy', or 'big bang', which emphasised the need for rapid and radical economic reforms (macroeconomic stabilisation, privatisation, price liberalisation, free trade) to be introduced immediately and thereby to lay the foundations for accelerated economic growth. At the other end of the transition policy spectrum was a 'gradualist' approach, which, although accepting the need for these measures, stressed the importance of the institutional and social aspects of the transition process as prerequisites for the successful and less painful implementation of the economic reforms (Fischer *et al.* 1996; Stiglitz 1999; World Bank 2000). In the main it was the 'shock therapy' school (some would describe it as 'blitzkrieg') which prevailed, with most of the CEECs speedily adopting macroeconomic stabilisation programmes designed to lower inflation and secure progress towards fiscal stability, while simultaneously liberating price controls and removing currency and trade restrictions. Perhaps the best depiction of the economic dislocations of the early transition years comes from Janos Kornai: it constituted a 'transformational recession' which captured the necessarily painful and evolutionary nature of the economic transition process, a process that almost certainly could not have been accomplished without considerable economic dislocations (Kornai 1993 and 2000).

The CEECs began to show signs of recovery from the beginning of 1994, with inflation moderating and the fiscal imbalance improving. Even then, however, this translated only into a slowing-down in the pace of economic decline rather than positive economic growth rates. As shown in Table 5.1, it was only by the end of the 1990s, and notwithstanding wide variation in the economic performance of the CEEC economies, that most of the CEECs managed to regain their pre-transition GDP levels.

By the end of the 1990s, therefore, only the Baltic states out of these countries continued to record GDP levels significantly below their pre-

Table 5.1 Selected transition characteristics of CEEC 10

Country	Year transition begins	Starting date of stabilisation programme	Real output ratio 1999/1989	Average inflation 1989–99
Czech Rep.	1991	Jan. 91	0.94	7.8
Hungary	1990	Mar. 90	0.99	19.7
Poland	1990	Jan. 90	1.28	49.2
Slovakia	1991	Jan. 91	1.01	14.3
Slovenia	1990	Feb. 92	1.05	12.9
Estonia	1992	Jun. 92	0.78	24.3
Latvia	1992	Jun. 92	0.56	35.1
Lithuania	1992	Jun. 92	0.70	41.0
Bulgaria	1991	Feb. 91	0.67	68.4
Romania	1991	Jan. 93	0.74	76.1

Source: IMF World Economic Outlook, 2000, Chapter III, p. 89.

reform levels, although only Poland had recorded any substantial economic growth over that decade. Since then, and doubtless as a consequence of the reform process nearing its completion, economic growth in most of the countries has averaged 3 per cent per annum, exceeding that recorded in the EU-15. However, notwithstanding the gradual recovery of output levels in these countries, there remained a considerable unemployment problem. In 2002, Poland, the largest country, recorded an unemployment rate of 20 per cent, the highest in any of the CEECs. Elsewhere, although levels were lower, unemployment remained a major problem.

In some respects this raw economic data looks surprisingly benign. Certainly unemployment is above the EU-average in most countries, but is no higher than, for instance, Spain recorded in the early 1990s. Similarly, we only need to go back to the 1996–7 recession to find comparable fiscal imbalances for the major EU-15 countries. Although inflation is well above the EU average, the sustained EU disinflation is a relatively recent phenomenon. However, this data excludes arguably the principal indicator of the economic state of the accession countries, namely per capita income. That data shows that, at best, the average per capita GDP in the eight CEEC accession counties is, at 45.6 per cent, less than half of the EU average, with the range extending from 34.8 per cent in Latvia to 69.6 per cent in Slovenia (the latter being close to the average per capita income in Greece).

An immediate problem this poses for the EU-15 is the future distribution of the EU structural funds, funds which currently benefit some of the weaker regions across the EU-15. However, the underlying political and economic problems revolve around the implications of the evolution of a twin-speed enlarged EU characterised by a strong and economically dynamic 'core' of modern, knowledge-based economies surrounded by a 'periphery' of economically weaker and disadvantaged countries, in which both economic growth and the accumulation of wealth is slower. What is already clear is that the growth 'premium', which the CEECs have enjoyed in the

Table 5.2 CEEC: basic economic data, 2003

	GDP (% change)	Unemployment (% of labour force)	Inflation (% change)	Fiscal balance (% of GDP)
Czech Rep.	2.8	7.7	1.5	−6.3
Hungary	3.7	6.2	5.0	−4.9
Poland	2.5	20.6	1.1	−4.2
Slovakia	3.7	18.2	8.8	−5.3
Slovenia	3.4	6.3	6.0	−1.5
Estonia	4.9	10.0	3.5	−0.5
Latvia	5.5	11.1	2.5	−2.9
Lithuania	4.5	16.2	1.0	−1.9

Source: European Commission, Directorate General for Enlargement.

past few years compared to the EU-15, is insufficient to result in a speedy catch-up of relative GDP levels. Indeed, estimates produced by the Economist Intelligence Unit in June 2003 suggest that GDP catch-up under benign assumptions about CEEC economic growth will require a weighted average period of 56 years before the CEECs average income levels converge to EU-15 levels.

The microeconomic dimension to enlargement

The microeconomic dimension to enlargement covers a range of economic effects that operate at the level of the enterprise or the environment within which the enterprise operates. We have noted already that the past decade has witnessed radical changes in the economic environment in the accession countries, following the implementation of reforms to give effect to the process of transition. At the same time, the impact of the liberalisation of trade between the accession countries and the EU-15 has not only had a marked effect on the structure of inter-area trade flows, but has also changed the competitive environment within which CEEC firms operate. In this section we review these effects under two headings. First, we will consider the orthodox trade and related gains, which economic theory predicts will accrue as barriers to trade and factor flows are eliminated between the EU-15 and the CEECs. Second, we will consider the policy aspect of enlargement, in particular focusing on the transitional arrangements that have been negotiated and which provide a period during which the CEECs will progressively assume the full obligations of EU membership. In that section, we consider in detail three specific dimensions to EU policy which have emerged as problematic in the enlargement negotiations: the impact on the EU budget; the common agricultural policy; and the impact of enlargement on the future of the structural funds.

EU enlargement and the gains from economic integration

Orthodox international trade theory predicts that the creation or enlarging of a customs union will generate two sets of economic effect. The first effect is 'static' and describes the once-and-for-all net resource allocation effects that will result from the elimination of barriers to trade between the participants in the customs union. As trade barriers are removed, economic theory predicts two sets of static effect, 'trade creation' and 'trade diversion'. Trade creation describes the new trade flows that are created because of the removal of trade barriers and the triggering of the forces of comparative advantage. Trade creation leads to an improved international allocation of resources and so to positive gains in economic welfare for all participants in the union. Trade diversion, on the other hand, is welfare-lowering, as this occurs when low cost imports to the customs union from non-members of the union are displaced by more costly, but now tariff-free, goods originating within the union. If trade creation exceeds trade diversion then the customs union is welfare-enhancing. Empirical studies over a range of cases of customs unions unanimously concur that the trade-creating gains substantially outweigh trade-diverting losses. Accordingly, enlargement is forecast to generate modest static gains to the EU as a whole in that the resulting increase in trade will produce a more efficient allocation of productive resources across the EU as a whole.

However, the static effects of enlargement do not exhaust the economic effects of EU enlargement. We must also factor in a range of dynamic effects triggered by the accession of the CEECs to the EU which are widely agreed to be economically more significant than the static effects. Typically, economists identify three sources of dynamic gain from integration: economies of scale; enhanced competition; and, more contentiously, intensified research and development activity. To this list, we would add a fourth source of dynamic gain, the impact of enlargement on international investment activity in the accession countries. The dynamic gains of enlargement can be expected to outweigh significantly the static effects both because of their recurring nature and the impact they will have on the rates of growth in both the accession countries and the region as a whole. First, the gains from economies of scale arise because of the fall in production costs that occur as companies increase the level of their output in order to service the now larger internal market. Assuming these gains are passed on to consumers in the form of lower prices, consumer welfare will rise accordingly as resources are allocated more efficiently. Second, competition will increase directly as firms from the new member states enter the enlarged 'internal' market. Once again, costs and prices will be reduced as inefficiencies are driven from the production and management process and, assuming competition policy is effective, this will generate further consumer benefits.

Third, it is arguable that enlarging the market will increase the quantity of resources allocated by companies to research and development activity (R&D). There are two possible mechanisms at work here: first, companies might increase the resources they assign to research and development activity, in the hope that they will generate innovations that increase their competitive edge and thus gain market share; and second, if companies grow larger, as they exploit the economies of scale associated with a larger domestic market, then they might opt to increase the resources they apply to R&D activities. The fourth and final source of dynamic gain is the impact that membership of a large internal market may have on flows of foreign direct investment (FDI). This is a particularly important matter in the context of the prospective enlargement of the EU. Table 5.3 gives data of FDI to the eight CEECs for a sample of years after 1994.

It is worth noting that by the end of the 1990s, FDI to the CEECs exceeded 5 per cent of their GDP. While the underlying dynamics of FDI flows are notoriously complex, the data in Table 5.3 suggest a crude relationship between three independent variables: degree of success in the

Table 5.3 Foreign direct investment inflows (US$m) to accession countries

	1994	1995	1996	1997	1998	1999	2000	2001	2002
Czech Republic	878	2,568	1,435	1,287	3,699	6,313	4,986	4,923	8,435
Estonia	214	202	150	266	581	305	387	539	307
Hungary	1,145	4,810	2,556	3,134	2,649	3,454	3,483	4,322	2,700
Latvia	214	180	382	521	357	348	410	164	396
Lithuania	31	73	152	355	926	487	379	446	732
Poland	1,875	3,659	4,498	4,908	6,365	7,270	9,341	5,713	4,900
Slovakia	270	235	351	174	561	355	2,053	1,475	4,012
Slovenia	117	151	174	334	216	107	136	503	1,865

Source: *Europe Enlarged: Understanding the Impact*, Economist Intelligence Unit, 2003.

economic transition process; proximity to the market 'core' of the EU; and probability of early EU accession. To this one would need to add such factors as wage rates and skill of labour force. Possibly the most striking feature of the data presented here is not the gradual increase in the flows of FDI as the date of accession grows nearer, but the situation with respect to Slovakia, a country that until February 2000 was not considered to be in the first wave of EU enlargement. With the decision that Slovakia would be included in the negotiations for early accession, FDI inflows increased sharply and have been sustained. There is little doubt that the economic convergence of the CEECs will greatly benefit from FDI, although future flows will rely on steady progress continuing to be made with regard to economic transition and domestic economic policies in the wake of enlargement.

It is clear that by the time enlargement occurs, many of the static and dynamic economic effects described above will already have impacted on the enlarged EU's economic system. The domestic economic reforms that took place in the CEECs during the 1990s, coupled with the liberalisation of trade flows between those countries and the EU-15 under the aegis of the Europe agreements, has meant that many of the economic adjustments outlined above have already had an opportunity to take place. For instance, the volume of EU-15 exports to the CEECs grew from 1989 to 1999 by a factor of 3.9 and the volume of imports from the CEECs to the EU-15 by a factor of 3.1, equivalent to annual average growth rates of 15 per cent and 12 per cent respectively over the period. As can be seen from Table 5.4, more than two-thirds of the CEEC accession country exports are already destined for EU-15 markets, while less than 10 per cent of EU extra area exports are destined for these markets.

If we consider the sectoral distribution of CEEC–EU trade, the Commission estimates that the EU has specialised in high-technology products while the CEEC provide products requiring lower-skilled labour and resource-intensive exports. Nonetheless, there is some evidence of growing intra-industry trade between the two groups, implying that over time the

Table 5.4 Trade between EU-15 and CEEC-8, 1994–1999

CEEC trade with EU	1994	1995	1996	1997	1998	1999
Exports to EU as % total exports	42.7	55.4	56.5	58.4	63.6	68.2
Imports from EU as % total imports	41.5	55.9	56.6	57.4	60.6	61.3
EU trade with CEECs	*1994*	*1995*	*1996*	*1997*	*1998*	*1999*
Exports to CEECs as % total extra-EU Exports	4.2	6.0	6.3	6.7	7.6	7.7
Imports from CEECs as % total extra-EU Imports	3.7	5.3	5.4	5.7	6.6	6.8

Source: The Economic Impact of Enlargement, European Commission, June 2001.

CEECs may well be able to move up the value-added chain and increase their share of skill- and knowledge-intensive production within an enlarged EU. Similarly, that study suggested that the domestic economic reforms undertaken by the CEECs in the past decade had resulted in increased FDI activity in those economies, although up to one-half of FDI flows had been directed to non-tradeable sectors such as public utilities. Of the remaining FDI, a significant part seems to have been motivated by a desire to increase market share in the CEEC itself, rather than for export substitution purposes.

Thus far we have discussed the effects of liberalisation of the movement of goods and services and of capital. A particularly difficult issue arises with regard to the 'fourth' freedom, namely the free movement of labour. Here, the dominant concern is on the part of the EU where there are fears that enlargement will lead to a migration of labour from the CEECs to the present member states. Not only does this raise the spectre of putting unsustainable pressures on the welfare systems in the present member states but also, to the extent that skilled labour participates in this type of migration, raises fears that it would adversely affect the economic development prospects of the CEECs themselves. However, the evidence from the period since 1990 does not suggest that there has been a significant net migration from the CEECs. In part, this is attributed to the restrictions which the EU put in place. At the same time, however, it may also reflect an initial exaggeration of the likely scale of labour movement. Current estimates suggest that only about 335,000 people would move from the CEECs to the present member states even if there were to be no controls on the free movement of workers post-enlargement. In fact the EU has agreed a seven-year transition phase for implementing this, during which time the east–west flow of labour will be limited.

Overall the evidence suggests that enlargement itself will not herald any dramatic change in the broad economic flows between the CEEC accession states and EU-15. Instead, we would expect the progressive integration between the CEEC economies and the EU-15 to continue to evolve, a process begun in the early 1990s as the liberalisation of cross-border trade and investment began to take effect. Indeed, a large part of the economic adjustment we would expect to follow trade liberalisation has already taken place, although in certain sensitive sectors such as agriculture, textiles and labour markets further adjustment is inevitable in the future as transition arrangements unwind. There will continue to be local adjustment problems therefore, as the gains in economic efficiency arising from enlargement have their effect on non-competitive producers. But such negative effects will be more than offset by the economic benefits accruing from a more efficient allocation of resources and the opportunities offered by an expansion of the internal market.

Finally, it is worth stressing that the microeconomic dimension to enlargement will continue to depend on the success of the economic reform process in the accession countries and on the evolution of economic conditions therein. In particular, efficiency conditions in production, along with the infrastructure available to enhance the transition to modern, knowledge-based economies, are crucial to the long-term economic prospects in all these countries. At present, foreign investment and domestic production are responding to the certainty of imminent access to the large, EU internal market. These forces are also responding to the competitive advantage that some of the accession countries presently enjoy, especially in the form of a comparatively low-wage and skilled labour force. It is perhaps inevitable that real wages in these accession countries will begin to experience upward pressure as the demand for labour rises and as workers themselves begin to demand higher wages in order to bring them closer to parity with their counterparts in the EU-15. In that event, competitiveness might suffer with the risk of slowing down what is already bound to be a gradual process of economic catch-up.

The obligations of membership

Although the Copenhagen criteria stipulated that CEEC candidates should be able to assume the obligations of EU membership before joining the EU, from the outset of the enlargement negotiations it was clear that certain aspects of the *acquis* could not be met other than over the very long term. Indeed, delaying enlargement unreasonably would risk undermining the economic and political reform process necessary if the *acquis* were ever to be fully implemented. Consequently, when the enlargement negotiations properly started, it was accepted that there would need to be lengthy transition periods in some areas. However, the EU-15 did insist that the accession countries should be able to take on the overwhelming part of the obligations arising from the operation of the single market ahead of membership, including the legal and administrative capacities required to implement attendant policies. Indeed, a large part of the financial support given to the accession states was, in the latter stages, explicitly geared to an institution-building facility. It is also worth noting that a specific safeguard clause has been included within the accession treaty to allow the Commission to take measures in case of problems.

In granting a transition period to the accession countries, this enlargement differs from previous enlargements only in terms of the sometimes longer time-frame during which compliance with EU legislative obligations must be achieved. Every enlargement thus far has extended to new members a period of transition. Nonetheless, derogations from EU obligations have only been agreed in a relatively few instances and the CEECs have agreed to meet the overwhelming part of the obligations arising from membership of the EU on entry. Typically these fixed-term derogations from EU obligations arise with respect to EU environmental obligations, where the cost of meeting EU standards is simply prohibitive; health and safety regulations at work; state aid regulations; a number of aspects of the CAP; transport policy; taxation; and some aspects of the free movement of capital and persons. In the matter of monetary union, there is no fixed-term derogation, as the time-frame involved depends on how quickly the accession states can fulfil the Maastricht convergence criteria.

Although only relatively few and well-justified, temporary derogations to EU obligations have been agreed, concern remains that the accession countries will find it difficult in practice to fulfil their obligations in several major policy areas. These concerns stem either from the apparent slow pace of requisite internal reforms in the accession countries themselves (including law-making and the transposition of EU law), or from a per-ceived weakness in the domestic administrative and judicial arrangements that are the essential infrastructure for the enforcement of EU rules: for example in the areas of public procurement; state aid to industry; competi-tion policy; financial services; protection of intellectual property rights; and workplace legislation.

Notwithstanding these broad, and sometimes deep-seated, concerns regarding the potential problems of enlargement such as administrative capacity and legislative timetable, there are additionally three policy areas in which particular difficulties have arisen during the accession negoti-ations and for which specific provisions have been agreed. These are agricultural policy, structural funds and the EU budget.

Agriculture

The Common Agricultural Policy (CAP) accounts for nearly half of total EU spending and despite recent reform continues to represent the major item of the budget. The problem in the enlargement negotiations was the large potential cost to the EU budget, and how this would be financed, should the level of price support available to EU-15 member states be made available to the accession countries. Many of the CEECs have relatively large and inefficient farm sectors in which significant numbers of the domestic workforce are dependent upon farming, as in Poland, where 25 per cent of the labour force is involved in agriculture. Unsurprisingly, the view from the accession states was that they should be entitled to support payments under the CAP, as are EU member states. The EU-15 position was against increasing the budget as required to meet the financial obligations that would arise under that scenario. Moreover, it was unwilling to cut payments to current beneficiaries in order to free monies to pay to farmers in the accession countries. Although motivated principally by the financial cost of extending the CAP, there was also concern on the EU-15 side that this would act as a disincentive to the implementation of much-needed farm modernisation programmes in the accession countries. The compromise that was negotiated involved a transition period of ten years (2004–13) during which farm support through direct payments in the accession countries would progressively be raised to EU-15 levels, although upon membership accession-country farmers would receive only 25 per cent of the current EU-15 level of CAP support. At the same time, some five billion euro for a rural development package was committed to the accession states at the December 2002 Copenhagen summit. Although the financial impact on the CAP arising from enlargement has been addressed, the long-term implications for the CAP remain uncertain. In part this is due to uncertainty about the speed of agricultural modernisation in the CEECs themselves. However, it also reflects on-going uncertainty about the future of the CAP, in particular the extent to which the decoupling of farm payments from farm production and other agreed reforms of the CAP are implemented. The outcome of the WTO Doha Development Round will be another important factor. It is also worth stressing that enlargement will strengthen and not weaken the EU's agricultural lobby, which is seeking to maintain farm subsidies at high levels.

Regional aid

Enlargement poses another considerable challenge in the field of EU structural actions. Enlargement will bring into the EU eight new member states that have an average GDP of less than 50 per cent of the EU average. Accordingly, under the existing structural fund legislation, each of the CEECs will be eligible for substantial support under the EU's structural funds, principally the European Regional Development Fund (Objective 1), the European Social Fund and also under the EU Cohesion Fund. As the legislative framework governing the structural funds coincides with the EU-15 financial perspective, which finishes at the end of 2006, the enlargement negotiations concerned only eligibility and financial commitments of the CEECs over the period 2004–6. The real debate over the future of the structural funds will only begin when the Commission publishes its proposals for the next financial perspective. The overall allocation for structural actions in the accession states for the period 2004–6 was set at 14.2 billion euro, of which over 93 per cent is designated to financing Objective 1 assistance. A further 7.5 billion euro has been allocated under the Cohesion Fund, almost half of which goes to Poland, in order to assist those countries achieve the fiscal pre-conditions for membership of the euro zone. The outstanding immediate concern on the part of the EU surrounds the capacity of the CEECs both to administer this assistance and to provide the requisite degree of domestic co-financing of programmes that are supported by the funds. Over the longer, post-2006, period, enlargement sets new challenges to the EU to achieve the degree of 'economic and social cohesion' to which it has long been committed. There are two principal problems. First, because of the low levels of GDP in the accession countries, enlargement necessarily will result in a fall in the average EU per capita income. This means that certain EU-15 regions currently eligible for structural fund support because their average per capita GDP is below 75 per cent of the EU average will find themselves no longer eligible and this may slow down the rate at which they are catching up with the EU's more prosperous regions. Second, this enlargement could create a possibly permanent division of the EU into a two-speed economy, in which the rich dynamic core becomes progressively wealthier and the less prosperous peripheral and underdeveloped regions become increasingly poorer, at least in relative terms. Should this occur, and the policy costs of avoiding this may prove politically unacceptable to the wealthier states, then the political solidarity of the EU may well become increasingly fragile. To avoid this, the enlarged EU might well have to increase significantly resources assigned to structural actions in the CEECs, although this would require that the rule, which prevents structural assistance exceeding 4 per cent of GDP be changed.

Budget

The final problem in the enlargement negotiations was, of course, the financial implications, on which agreement was reached in agriculture, and a package covering the budget and the structural funds. The final deal did not satisfy all the CEECs but they had little choice but to accept it. Another major negotiation can be expected over the future budget of the enlarged Union. The current budget expires at the end of 2006 and before that we can expect a series of intense discussions on the future of EU spending policies, in which the fundamental division will be between the net contributors to the EU budget, the richer members, and the net beneficiaries, the poorer members, Within the latter group there will be a further division between the 'old' net beneficiaries of Greece, Spain,

Portugal and the 'new' ones joining in 2004. In addition, matters will be further complicated by the impending membership of the EU of both Bulgaria and Romania, expected in 2007, and possibly Croatia and, later, Turkey. It is impossible to forecast how the next budget debate will unfold as the Commission has not yet produced the proposal on which the discussions will be based. However, the central questions will revolve around (a) the future of the structural funds, (b) the pace of CAP reforms, and (c) the financial ceiling which stipulates that the EU budget cannot exceed 1.27 per cent of EU GDP.

The macroeconomic dimension to enlargement

In this section we examine the macroeconomic dimension to enlargement. First, we review the degree of economic convergence between the CEECs and EU over the period since 1993 and the prospects for the future. Second, we consider the likely impact of enlargement on prospects for EU economic ambitions, as manifest in the Lisbon agenda.

While the majority of EU-15 countries continue to experience weak economic growth, with some such as Germany being close to recession conditions, the economic prospects for the CEECs look to be comparatively favourable. Based largely on the continued strength of domestic demand, the rate of economic growth in these countries averaged 2.9 per cent in 2002, and is expected to be above 3 per cent in both 2003 and 2004, considerably ahead of the 1.3 per cent and 2.4 per cent growth that is currently forecast for the EU in these two years. At the same time, this growth is accompanied by a decline in annual inflation rates across the CEECs and these conditions hold out the prospect of a 'virtuous economic' cycle being triggered. The rate of inflation in the CEECs has fallen sharply in recent years, although with an average of almost 3 per cent in 2002–3 it remains above the EU average (currently below 2 per cent). In large measure this reduced inflation is attributed to a lower imported component in inflation due to a combination of cheaper imports, reflecting the near-recession conditions in the EU, and the appreciation of some CEEC currencies against the US dollar. Wage inflation, on the other hand, continues to be a problem in the accession countries, with money wage increases running ahead of productivity gains thus producing a sharp rise in real wages and, accordingly, unit costs of production. Curtailing inflationary forces therefore continues to present a challenge to the CEECs. In the short term, currency movements between these countries and the EU will offer a mechanism for offsetting this loss in the cost competitiveness of CEEC exports. However, should currency stability become a priority for the CEECs once they have joined the EU, this route will be closed and any loss in price competitiveness will be manifest in falling demand and output.

Unemployment is a severe problem in some of the accession countries, with the largest, Poland, recording a rate of unemployment in excess of 20 per cent in 2003. To an extent, unemployment in the accession countries, particularly Poland, rose as the enterprise restructuring necessary to meet the EU *acquis* intensified in the latter stages of the enlargement negotiations. In addition to this 'transformational' element, increases in the labour supply and adverse cyclical factors have contributed to raising the rate of unemployment in some of the accession states.

The principal macroeconomic problem confronting the CEECs relates to fiscal policy and in particular to the current scale of government budget deficits in these countries. With the exception of the Baltic states, each of the accession states has a budget deficit in excess of 3 per cent, the post-Maastricht benchmark for EU countries to achieve ahead of membership of the euro zone. During 2003, the budget deficit in Hungary exceeded 9 per cent GDP, while in Poland, the Czech Republic and Slovakia the deficit was around 5 per cent of GDP. In Poland this could easily rise further if governments increase public spending in an attempt to fuel economic growth.

Two further complications are likely to arise. First, it is inevitable that EU membership will place further upward strains on public spending to the extent that CEEC authorities are required to match EU spending under structural actions with domestic resources and finance public investment projects that are required to implement the EU *acquis* (e.g. in the area of environmental policy). Some part of this may be met by higher taxes and/or borrowing, although both these options risk either a decline in consumer and investor spending directly or as a result of upward pressures on interest rates. Second, macroeconomic policy in the accession states will need to be increasingly geared to meeting the Maastricht fiscal criteria, if they are to achieve their stated goal of being in the euro zone by 2006–9. Failure to make headway towards greater fiscal consolidation might well lead to investor uncertainty and exchange rate instability, with adverse consequences for exports and FDI. An excessively zealous fiscal austerity programme, however, could easily curtail the level of domestic activity and undermine the positive growth prospects these countries currently enjoy. It is the case that some of the underlying causes of the fiscal imbalances in the accession states are transitory in nature, such as the up-front costs of pension and health care reforms and the high costs of economic restructuring. However, others might well be structural in nature and will require deliberate policy changes to affect them. The accession countries have a tradition of relatively generous state-funded social welfare payments, and these may well have to be reformed in the medium term. Also, revenue collection in the CEECs is notoriously problematic and this requires policy changes.

The macroeconomic outlook for the CEECs, while relatively favourable, clearly carries attendant risks that could undermine the dynamics of real economic convergence between these countries and the EU-15, a process already likely to take decades to achieve. There is a danger that simultaneously pursuing real economic convergence and monetary convergence (to join the euro zone), will lead to a domestic policy conflict. This is because three of the four Maastricht EMU criteria (price stability relative to best performing euro zone countries, exchange rate stability and convergence of long-term interest rates to those in the euro zone's best-performing inflation countries) are linked directly to monetary policy. Changes in interest rates in an effort to achieve the Maastricht criteria could run counter to the monetary policy needs of the real economy. Thus, while the room for manoeuvre of domestic economic policy is greater now than before, it remains somewhat restricted by the under-performing real economies of the accession countries.

At the same time, EU membership itself will spur economic growth in the CEECs (Kok 2003). The effects of this will be maximised to the extent that the economic reform process in the accession states continues along its current trajectory and that fiscal consolidation continues within a benign inflationary environment. In turn, this could lead to a lowering of the costs of CEEC borrowing as interest rates come into line with euro zone averages. A study in 2001 by the European Commission estimated that enlargement could increase the growth of GDP of the accession states by between 1.3 and 2.1 percentage points annually and for the EU-15 it could increase the level of GDP by 0.7 percentage points on a cumulative basis. Enlargement will also impact on the economic governance of the EU. Most directly this will impact on the European Central Bank, although the full implications for the ECB will not arise until the accession states join the euro zone. At the same time, the accession states will need to agree convergence programmes with the European Commission that detail measures designed to meet the EMU membership criteria.

Enlargement and the Lisbon process

At the Lisbon European Council in March 2000, EU leaders pledged to create 'the most competitive and dynamic knowledge-based economy in the world by 2010'. This pledge triggered what has come to be known as the 'Lisbon process', a phrase that describes the wide range of techniques, from orthodox legislation to 'benchmarking' and peer review of performance, that is being used in many economic and social policy arenas to implement this vision. Ultimately, the process of economic reform seeks to intensify competition, reform labour markets, strengthen economic and social cohesion and ensure consistency between economic and environmental aims. Enlargement will set the Lisbon process a severe series of tests, although it is clear that, in any event, the EU-15 are failing to make satisfactory progress in achieving their goals. Nonetheless, enlargement will make it even more difficult for some of the Lisbon targets to be met, such as raising the overall workforce participation rate to 70 per cent, fully completing the internal market in the areas of telecoms, energy and financial services and raising research and development spending to 3 per cent of GDP. The difficulty facing the accession states is two-fold: first, prioritising the Lisbon strategy will require that scarce financial resources are deflected from other, possibly more beneficial, uses, and second, that the measures needed to achieve certain goals on the Lisbon agenda will conflict with other objectives of domestic economic policy. So while the broad tenets of the Lisbon strategy will undoubtedly contribute to economic growth and employment in the accession states just as much as in the EU-15, it is less likely that the former will be able to adhere to a schedule that has been established for the prosperous mature market economies of the EU-15. It is less clear if enlargement will have any adverse impact on the reform process in the EU-15. Indeed, somewhat ironically the CEECs arguably are well placed to advise on the implementation of 'transformational' reforms of the type implicit in the Lisbon strategy.

Conclusion

This chapter has focused on the economic aspect of enlargement with particular reference to the accession of the eight central and east European countries. We have suggested that in large measure many of the economic impacts that are associated with countries joining an existing customs union (the EU) have, in this case, already taken effect. The enlargement of the EU on this occasion has, in practical economic terms, been on-going since the early 1990s. Therefore we do not expect any dramatic trade effects or adjustment problems to surface after 1 May 2004. The economic problems that do remain are within the arena of EU economic and social policies and the local costs and administrative infrastructures that are necessary to implement and enforce the EU *acquis*. At the same time, particular problems surround the macroeconomic policies of the accession states, especially with respect to the appropriate fiscal and monetary policy mix in the context of securing real economic convergence on the one hand, and the monetary and fiscal policy convergence necessary to join the euro zone on the other hand. As we have suggested, conflict in this matter is a distinct risk over the next decade.

Unarguably the dominant dilemma which this enlargement poses to the political economy of the EU involves the inclusion of eight countries that are substantially poorer in economic terms than the average of the current EU-15. The overwhelming part of the economic evidence available suggests that, even in benign economic circumstances, it will take decades for the new states to catch up in GDP terms with the EU average. This sets profound economic policy challenges to the EU in so far as it continues to espouse the importance of achieving a deeper integration characterised by a high level of 'economic and social cohesion'. We will gain some insight into the degree of determination of the EU to accelerate the real economic convergence process in the negotiations on the next budget period. If, as seems likely, the wealthier members of the EU are unwilling to increase significantly the redistributive elements of the budget, then we would predict that the current enlargement of the EU will be accompanied by an intensification in political pressures, especially given the possibility of the emergence of an economically divided, two-speed Union. While there are no doubts that economic gains, both internally and with respect to the EU as an international economic actor, are likely to accrue with enlargement, the domestic consequences arising from potential problems of a failure of internal cohesion and solidarity cannot be understated.

References

Commission of the European Communities (2001) *The Economic Impact of Enlargement,* Brussels: European Commission Directorate General for Economic and Financial Affairs.

Commission of the European Communities (2002) *Towards the Enlarged Union,* COM(2002) 700, Brussels: European Commission.

Economist Intelligence Unit (2003) *Europe Enlarged: Understanding the Impact,* London: Economist Intelligence Unit.

Fisher, S., Sahay, R. and Vegh, C.A. (1996) 'Stabilization and growth in transition economies: the early experience', *Journal of Economic Perspectives* (Spring), pp. 45–66.

Kok, W. (2003) *Enlarging the European Union: Achievements and Challenges,* Florence: European University Institute.

Kornai, J. (1993) *Transformational Recession. A General Phenomenon Examined through the Example of Hungary's Development,* Budapest: Institute for Advanced Study, Discussion Paper No. 1, June.

Kornai, J. (2000) 'Ten years after "The Road to a Free Economy": the author's self-evaluation', paper for the World Bank Annual Conference on Development Economics, Washington.

Stiglitz, J. (1999) 'Whither reform', paper presented to the World Bank Annual Conference on Development Economics, Washington.

World Bank (2000) *World Economic Outlook 2000,* Chapters III, IV, Washington, DC: World Bank.

Further reading

Scott, A. (2002) 'Theories of regional economic integration and the global economy', in Gower, J. (ed.) *The European Union Handbook,* second edition, London: Fitzroy Dearborn.

6 The Wider Europe

Geoffrey Harris

Summary

Fifteen years after the event, the Union is still coming to terms with the consequences of the reunification of Germany and the collapse of communism, which began with the revolutionary changes of 1989. Many European countries are not in the EU but their development is very much influenced by the Union and its policies. The enlargement process continues with new members contributing their specific experiences and outlooks. Several countries, particularly in central and south-eastern Europe, plan to join the EU and the Union is being obliged to clarify its response to the various groups of countries concerned. These responses come under the heading of the Wider Europe and in July 2003 the Commission established a task force to deal with the policy implications. At present, the future frontiers of the EU cannot, therefore, be predicted.

Introduction

The fact that the EU now has to consider further membership applications and to redefine its relationships with its neighbours provides another challenge, a 'problem' generated by the very success and attractiveness of a Union which has become the principal source of, and framework for, prosperity and security in the region.

Some observers were already speaking in 2003 of 'enlargement fatigue' but such judgements are likely to prove premature in the wake of the important policy statement, adopted by the Council on 18 November 2002:

1 With the forthcoming biggest ever enlargement in its history, the EU will have borders with a number of new neighbours. Enlargement presents an important opportunity to take forward relations with the new neighbours of the EU, which should be based on shared political and economic values.

2 In particular, the EU wishes to put in place further conditions, which would allow it to enhance its relations with its Eastern European

neighbours: Ukraine, Moldova and Belarus. There is a need for the EU to formulate an ambitious, long-term and integrated approach towards each of these countries, with the objective of promoting democratic and economic reforms, sustainable development and trade, thus helping to ensure greater stability and prosperity at and beyond the new borders of the Union.

3   The initiative will be based on a differentiated approach considering each country's distinct political and economic situation, potential and aims. The development of relations with the countries concerned will, of course, depend on their implementation of further reforms and their willingness to respect international commitments and common values on democracy, the rule of law and human rights.

4   This initiative should be seen in conjunction with the EU's strong commitment to deepening cooperation with the Russian Federation, which is a key partner.

5   The EU also encourages the further development of cross-border cooperation, including the fight against organised crime and illegal immigration, and regional cooperation with and among neighbouring countries in Eastern Europe. Furthermore, cooperation with relevant international organisations in the area, such as OSCE and the Council of Europe, will be an important element in the implementation of the initiative. In this respect, Candidate countries will play an important role.

(General Affairs Council, 18 November 2002)

This official commitment to pursue a Wider Europe policy inevitably raised questions about the EU's future borders. Mark Mazower of the University of London has written:

Just as the enlargement of the Union consigns the old 'European Europe' of the original six to the scrap heap of the past, so it raises the question of where Europe's limits should now be set. In the old days, the EU did not concern itself much with relations with its eastern neighbours; these involved matters it was happy to leave to its protecting superpower. Today, however, as political tensions rise around the Mediterranean and the Black Sea, this introverted approach no longer suffices. Today the EU has every reason to take more responsibility for what happens on and beyond its borders. The test case is now the EU's treatment of Turkey, where there is a new government in Ankara whose evolving relationship with its own religious inheritance is more than a little reminiscent of the dilemmas facing those eminently 'European' Christian Democrats half a century ago. The cold war is over and notions of an essentially Christian Europe need to be left behind, too, if the EU is to replicate the success in the next 50 years that it has enjoyed in the last.

(*Financial Times*, 12 December 2002: 21)

Media coverage of the conclusion of the accession negotiations with ten countries in December 2002 was overshadowed by the EU leaders' difficulties in deciding how to respond to the insistence of Turkey, supported by the US, on the definition of a target date for the opening of accession negotiations. Silvio Berlusconi, the prime minister of Italy, was satisfied with the decision taken on this matter but went much further, declaring that he was in favour of a Europe that incorporated Moldova, Ukraine, Belarus and the Russian Federation. He saw Israel also as a future EU member state. Romano Prodi was equally eloquent if more cautions in his choice of words, confirming that 'the enlargement process will not stop here' and announcing that the Commission would publish a communication early in 2003 with the aim of initiating a genuine debate. He referred to his view that the EU needed to create a 'circle of friends from Russia to the Black Sea and to the south of the Mediterranean' (*Agence Europe*, 14 December 2002). In a letter to the European Council on 21 January 2003, he added that in looking at the areas which would henceforth be part of the Union's immediate neighbourhood, the Commission would not suggest a new contractual framework but would propose to use existing instruments to give new impetus to Union policy towards the Mediterranean and the Balkans. He mentioned again that the Mediterranean countries should be seen as a 'linchpin' in our policy to create a 'ring of friends' around the new borders of the enlarged Union ranging from Morocco through the Black Sea to Russia. The imagery is a little confusing as there is no ring and to see Russia, Israel and Morocco even as part of a coherent arc or crescent is unconvincing (see Figure 6.1).

Words can be powerful political instruments, especially, when there can be a subtle difference between such concepts as proximity, neighbourhood, Wider Europe, European reunification and EU accession. There is no need to define the EU's political frontiers in advance. They will define themselves as the EU responds to each wave of accession applications. In the 1990s, France, Germany and others actively encouraged Poland and others to see their destiny in the EU. Messages coming from the EU to its neighbours can be important and have a bigger domestic political impact inside these countries than EU leaders and officials realise.

The EU's ring of friends

The 'ring of friends' is certainly a reassuring image and it reflects a specifically European concept of peace and security. In the Mediterranean in particular, this proves to be a fruitful way of engaging countries whose populations are increasingly hostile to 'the West', and encouraging them also on the road to regional cooperation as the main source of the kind of durable peace and economic development that Europe itself has achieved.

If Prodi's vision of a circle of friends contributing to Europe's peace and prosperity is to be a success, the EU will have to reaffirm its interest,

Figure 6.1 Map of Europe.

achievements and values in a way which could easily lead to clashes with American policy-makers who seem to concentrate on military aspects of security. But if the EU's neighbourhood is to be stabilised, cooperation with the US is necessary. The Stability Pact for the Balkans was launched in July 1999 in the presence of President Clinton as well as the leaders of the region and many other European countries. This contributed to its relative success, which has opened up the prospect of EU enlargement to the western Balkans.

Partnership around the Mediterranean

The Barcelona process, designed to strengthen ties between the EU and the countries of the Mediterranean, was launched in 1995 and includes twelve countries. Two of them, Cyprus and Malta, join the Union on 1 May 2004, and Turkey is also a candidate for EU membership. The others are

Algeria, Egypt, Israel, Jordan, Lebanon, Morocco, Syria, Tunisia and the Palestinian Authority. Libya, Mauritania and the Arab League regularly attend meetings as observers. The relationship between these countries and the EU is based on three levels of partnership: political and security; economic and financial; social and cultural. Since 1995, the EU has negotiated a new set of bilateral agreements with its partners. Relatively ambitious Euro-Med association agreements have replaced the previous cooperation agreements, but it is important to note that the process combines bilateral and multilateral elements. The EU also established the MEDA programme, which in its first decade will have disbursed over 10 billion euro, mostly for bilateral assistance, with 10 per cent for regional and sub-regional projects. As with the PHARE programme and the Europe agreements with the CEECs, political and economic conditionality is included in the rules.

Although Article 2 of the various association agreements provides a legal basis for 'appropriate measures' in the event of a serious breach of human rights, in fact there are no regular assessments of the development of human rights in the Euro-Med countries, or the kind of benchmarking applied in the annual progress reports presented by the Commission on the candidates for EU membership. If the EU wishes to strengthen stability in its neighbourhood, it might be wise now to upgrade the importance given to such issues and to raise them regularly and forcefully in the framework of political dialogue. The MEDA programme could draw on the experience of the PHARE and TACIS programmes and provide backing to projects linked to the development of civil society. Precisely because of the profound disillusionment in these countries with US foreign policy, the timing would seem propitious for this kind of democratic conditionality to be extended by the EU towards the countries of the Mediterranean.

The power of conditionality naturally varies in relation to the expectations of each partner country and its ability to achieve its goals without accepting EU offers or the conditions attached to them. Since 1993 it has become clear, for example, that the first of the Copenhagen criteria for EU accession, democracy and the rule of law, is a precondition for opening accession negotiations. For this reason, amongst others, Turkey has not yet achieved its ambition to get EU accession negotiations started but it received a clear message in Copenhagen in 2002 that its chances of doing so depended on further, substantial advances in the process of reforms already under way. At the other extreme, Israel gives priority to national security and seeks to achieve this objective in a way which is increasingly alien to the EU. The Union's power to influence is less, since Israel does not seek EU membership nor does it rely so much on trade and financial cooperation with the Union. Moreover, if the Union were to apply certain elements of democratic conditionality to Israel, it would have to act in a similar fashion towards other Euro-Med partner countries, for example Syria. Such a policy of inaction in relation to fundamental issues is likely to be reassessed as the Union expands. The newly acceding countries have had a decade of experience of constitutional reform, development of civil society and new forms of governance. They will be unlikely to support the continuing grant of billions of euros to countries not prepared to undertake reforms.

The Euro-Med partnership is based on the goal of establishing a free trade area by 2010. Many Arab countries feel that they receive too little attention and resources as compared with the post-communist countries. But the EU cannot ignore the fact that, in spite of financial aid received, the Arab countries have not implemented major economic and political reforms. The Wider Europe policy of the EU already includes special arrangements for multilateral political dialogue: Euro-Med with the south and the European Conference with the east and south-east. The EU, in contributing to the stability of its neighbourhood, also needs to build on its experience of resolving conflicts in ethnically complex societies. As one expert argues, 'The EU has become accustomed now to developing long-term comprehensive and evolutionary contractual relationships with all its neighbours' (Emerson and Tocci 2003: 145).

This approach of regional cooperation as the basis of peace and economic development could be extended to other Arab countries, but it is unlikely that this will be achieved unless the US, with its dominant role in relation to Israel and now Iraq, can see the value of such efforts. In the weeks and months after the fall of Baghdad, the war of words between some EU leaders and elements of the US administration might have led observers to overestimate the differences of outlook and interest between Europe and the US. Both have an overwhelming interest in regional security in the wider Middle East and both are committed by the nature of their societies to democracy, the rule of law and the market economy. America neither expects nor is it expected to involve itself in the day-to-day development of peace and democracy in the region, but for Europeans the situation is different. Cyprus is only 70 kilometres from Syria and Malta is only 200 kilometres from Libya. The EU will be too close to an explosive region to ignore its importance and it will be a real test not just for the EU's ambitions in terms of foreign and security policy but also in terms of its need for a stable 'ring of friends' on its borders.

The examples mentioned here also serve to confirm that the issue of stability in the wider sense is not just a question of further enlargement. Of the Euro-Med countries, Turkey is the only candidate for membership, after the accession of Cyprus and Malta. It would, however, be inappropriate to ignore totally the call for eventual EU membership for Israel mentioned by Bibi Nethanyahu during the 2002 Israeli general election. In May 2003 Israel's foreign minister Silvan Shalom told a visiting EP delegation that, although he was not preparing a formal application, he did think 'that a possibility exists for Israel to join the EU, since Israel and Europe share similar economies and democratic values' (Reuters, 20 May 2003). Mr Shalom's approach has been partially echoed by the former

Polish foreign minister, Bronislaw Geremek. The latter called for the eventual accession of both Israel and Palestine in what would be the mother of all conflict resolution achievements by the EU. During the course of the Convention many participants emphasised the Judaeo-Christian roots of European civilisation, so to have the land of Moses and Jesus inside the EU cannot be considered as unimaginable. It might also turn out that if and when Turkey moves closer to EU membership, the idea of balancing a new influx of Muslim EU citizens with membership for Israel could prove appealing in some quarters, especially in the light of the fact that Israel and Turkey have always been allies.

Turkey

The prospects for Turkey's accession remain unclear. In December 2002 the new government of Turkey invested much time, unsuccessfully, in trying to convince the European Council to fix a date for the opening of accession negotiations. In December 2004 European leaders will have to make a decision on this matter, on the basis of a report by the Commission on Turkey's progress towards meeting the criteria for EU membership. The Commission's report will be followed by a resolution setting out the views of the EP. During 2003 Turkey appeared to be gaining more sympathy and understanding in both institutions as well as from member states. Two issues could, however, still hold back Turkey's progress, the most important one being the continuing political role of the army. Leaving aside the precise institutional arrangements, which are unique for a European country, the role of the army was reported rather negatively when the UN efforts to achieve a solution to the Cyprus problem broke down early in 2003. According to the *Economist* (12 April 2003: 32), the prime minister, Tayyip Erdogan, was in the process of persuading the Turkish-Cypriot leader Rauf Denktash to sign the peace plan put forward by UN secretary general Kofi Annan when 'the generals, who cherish the island's northern part as a strategic asset, promptly slapped him down'. Equally relevant is the fact that, in the weeks preceding this setback, increasingly confident crowds had been gathering in the towns of northern Cyprus demanding that Denktash accept the Kofi Annan peace plan. They did so brandishing the European flag as a symbol of their defiance and their hopes. During the Iraq crisis of the spring of 2003, the Turkish military also seemed more cooperative with the US than did the Turkish political authorities but it remains to be seen whether the consistent support of Washington for Turkey's accession to the EU will continue. There are many other issues which will test Turkey's readiness for EU membership. Some Europeans believe that, as a Moslem country, Turkey has no place in the future of the EU. The fact remains that since 1999 Turkey has been treated as a candidate by the EU. It receives increasing amounts of 'pre-accession' financial assistance and everyone from the right to the left and from nationalist politicians to Kurdish leaders fully believes that Turkey should be in the European Union.

The western Balkans – moving towards European integration?

In its second progress report on the Stabilisation and Association Process (SAP) for south-eastern Europe (COM 139 2003: 15–16), the Commission stated that amongst its main messages 'the European Union confirms its commitment to the region and supports its continuing rapprochement with the Union'. A credible perspective of EU membership creates a powerful incentive for fundamental reform of these societies. The EU is clear and unambiguous about that perspective. At the same time it must be stressed that ultimate responsibility lies with the countries of the western Balkans themselves. Progress will depend on their will to introduce necessary reforms and to adopt European standards and values. There are no short cuts to European integration. The Commission also recalled that the SAP was a strategy for accession which will be achieved by each country on its own merits and in line with the speed of its progress. In many ways this approach reflects the experience of the most recent accessions. Agreed objectives, common criteria, individual merits and an accession target date are possible only once it is clear that progress has been achieved.

Again, the EU is putting a lot of money into the process, largely through the Community Assistance for Reconstruction, Development and Stabilisation (CARDS) programme. Given the history of the region, this programme includes aid to refugees but otherwise the priorities are similar to the PHARE programme, with the emphasis on the development of infrastructure and democratic stabilisation. In the report quoted above (COM 139 2003: 7), the Commission refers to the behaviour of politicians (confrontational approaches, personal agendas, corruption, obstruction and obfuscation) as an obstacle on their countries' road to the EU. The Commission also mentions the tendency in the region 'to politicise parliamentary administrations' as a sign of inadequate democratic development. By linking pressure for reform and financial assistance with the prospect of accession to the EU, the Union is applying the 'enlargement method' to the western Balkans. Members of the European Parliament have also been willing to speak in the same critical terms.

With Albania, the Union launched the negotiations for a Stabilisation and Association Agreement (SAA) on 31 January 2003, though for most of the preceding two years there had been high level official contacts and discussions within the Union on draft negotiating directives. However, the Council decided that the mandate for the Commission to start negotiations would only be adopted after the summer of 2003 and that opening accession negotiations would, therefore, depend on the political stability and domestic reforms in Albania.

Bosnia and Herzegovina (BiH) is following the same road. The next stage will be a feasibility report assessing whether BiH is ready to open negotiations for a SAA. The Commission argues that the country is still not a self-sustaining political and economic structure and remains too dependent on international assistance. A low turnout in the October 2002 general elections and the failure to deliver indicted war criminals to the International Criminal Tribunal for Yugoslavia (ICTY) in The Hague are amongst the challenge that BiH faces in trying to meet the basic democratic criteria for EU membership.

Serbia and Montenegro is in a similar situation. In its 2003 report the Commission does not even mention preparation of a feasibility study for a SAA, but sends a clear political message (p. 34) that 'EU efforts, even on the scale of recent years, cannot substitute for a lack of political will within the state'. The Commission states that leaving aside such tragedies as the murder of the pro-European reformer, prime minister Zoran Djindjic and the continuing lack of cooperation with the ICTY, progress in building stable, efficient and credible institutions has been slower than hoped. The 'final status' of Kosovo will also have to be resolved. A qualitative leap forward will be needed if this country is to benefit from the SAP and follow the road to EU accession. The new prime minister, Zoran Zivkovic, caused some consternation when he announced on a visit to Brussels that his country planned to apply for membership in 2004 (*Euractiv*, 21 May 2003). Mr Prodi and Mr Solana told him such expectations were 'hyper-optimistic', to which his response was 'we were told the same in 1999 when we said we would oust Milosevic from power, and yet we did it'.

Macedonia (officially the Former Yugoslav Republic of Macedonia, FYROM) also plans an early application for EU membership and its experience confirms that the road to EU membership is possible in spite of dramatic, even violent, political confrontations within the state. Its SAA was signed in Luxembourg on 9 April 2001, but this historic step was followed by renewed ethnic confrontation. The EU and NATO helped resolve this crisis and provided the security for Macedonia to resume normal political life and look to its European future.

In terms of EU membership, Croatia is the most ambitious country in the region, having presented its application for EU membership in February 2003. Its SAA was signed in October 2001 but ratification has been slow, due to a feeling in some member states that Croatia has been insufficiently cooperative with the ICTY. Croatia, for its part, considers that its 'homeland war' was a defensive response to Serbia's genocidal ambitions.

The result of the delays in ratification has been to undermine confidence in the SAA process and to open up the risk of renewed instability in the region. The fact that the agreements with FYROM and Croatia had not entered into force two years after their signature is a regrettable example of how national governments undermine EU policy in a region where instability has been endemic. Hopefully, as the Union enlarges, the member states will understand that a coherent regional strategy is put at risk if each member pursues its own national agenda.

Croatia's ambition to join the EU along with Bulgaria and Romania in 2007 may prove over-optimistic. In terms of its domestic preparations Croatia plans to be ready for EU membership by the end of 2006. The Commission is likely to recommend the opening of accession negotiations in the spring of 2004.

In May 2003 the Commission announced that European integration partnerships would be proposed for each country so that their pre-accession efforts would be monitored and encouraged with increased financial support. A Commission Communication of 21 May 2003 stated that

> the preparation of the countries of the western Balkans for future integration into European structures is a major priority of the European Union. These countries should have a clear perspective of joining the European Union when they have satisfied all the necessary criteria.

In Thessalonica on 21 June 2003 the future Europe was foreshadowed at the EU–Western Balkans Summit which brought together what could be the future EU of 33 member states. The message was that it is now up to the future candidates in the region to respond to the confidence shown in them by the Union, by advancing on the road to reform. The European Council confirmed that 'the Balkans will be an integral part of a unified Europe'. The purpose of the new 'enriched' EU partnership with these countries was to establish clear benchmarks to assess progress and lay the basis for a policy of conditionality in relation to increased financial assistance and the prospect of accession negotiations.

It has often been said that the 2004 enlargement of the EU heals the East–West division of Europe following the Second World War. In the same way, enlargement to the south-east would serve to heal the consequences of the First World War and the Treaty of Versailles. As Mark Mazower has pointed out, with the emergence of a united Germany and a united Italy 'nineteenth century nationalism had welded together tiny antiquated statelets into larger and economically more rational units; in the Balkans the outcome had been the opposite, resulting in a panoply of small, unviable, mutually antagonistic and internally intolerant states' (Mazower 2000: 4–5). To remedy this situation, EU enlargement into this region is as necessary and imaginative as the foundation of the Union itself in the 1950s.

The EU's eastern question – new neighbours or future members?

In Eastern Europe are other countries whose leaders also see EU accession as their national goal. In Ukraine, Belarus and Moldova, political instability is such that there are substantial questions over the functioning of democracy, which leads to doubts about the legitimacy of the leaders in place. However, civil society is developing in these countries and the movements and parties trying to advance this process see accession to the European Union as part of their attempts to modernise their societies.

With Russia, Ukraine, Belarus and Moldova, cooperation is in the form of Partnership and Cooperation Agreements (PCAs), which are bilateral treaties concluded for a period of ten years and provide the basis for the political, economic and trade relationship with the EU. The PCAs do not grant trade preferences, nor do they provide a timetable or framework for facilitating trade through approximation of partner countries' legislation to that of the EU's single market. The agreements with Russia, Ukraine and Moldova are in force. Negotiations for a PCA with Belarus were completed in March 1995 but they have not entered into force because of doubts about the democratic legitimacy of the regime of President Lukashenko. According to a survey carried out in the second half of 2000, the mass publics in these states are warmly disposed towards 'Europe' and the segment of opinion that can be identified as most democratic is most strongly European (White *et al.* 2002: 135–53).

The EU is clear in not expecting new membership applications from this region. The rhetoric, and the texts are clearly distinct from the message of Thessalonica. Indeed, on 16 June 2003, the EU's foreign ministers meeting in Luxembourg stated

> the EU wishes to define an ambitious new range of policies towards its neighbours based on shared values such as liberty, democracy, respect for human rights and fundamental freedoms, and the rule of law. This should be seen as separate from the question of possible EU accession that is regulated by article 49 of the Treaty on European Union.

In all the countries concerned, the EU institutions have had reasons to criticise the governments over such fundamental issues as violations of democracy and human rights, corruption and failure to meet commitments made to the EU. After enlargement, the EU's policy towards these countries could develop quickly. It is interesting to note that shortly after the European Council in Thessalonica had clarified EU policy towards its neighbours, four of the acceding countries (Poland, Slovakia, the Czech Republic and Hungary) meeting on 23 June 2003 expressed their explicit support for Ukraine's accession to the EU and offered their support and experience to their neighbour in achieving this ambition. There is danger here that premature talk of EU accession could provide support for leaders not genuinely committed to a European model of civil society. In this sense the situation in Ukraine, Belarus and Moldova remains different from the western Balkans countries where a clear choice has been made followed by a genuine commitment to get ready for EU accession.

Commission proposals

In a Communication on the Wider Europe–New Neighbour Initiative on 11 March 2003, the Commission argued (p. 5) that whilst 'enlargement has proved to be the Union's most successful foreign policy instrument . . . a response to the practical issues posed by proximity and neighbourhood should be seen as separate from the question of EU accession'. The EU's relations with the Mediterranean countries and the 'new outsiders' were, therefore, to be placed in a different perspective from those for the western Balkans. The Commission suggested a goal whereby (p. 14) the neighbouring countries ultimately had close political and economic links resembling those enjoyed within the EEA. But is it realistic to offer the same opportunities and expect the same standards of behaviour from Egypt and Ukraine, or from Belarus and Syria? The Commission also sees differentiation as remaining the basis for the new neighbourhood policy. It suggests that as the separate agreements with particular countries become fully implemented they should be replaced by a new instrument known as 'neighbourhood agreements'. In July 2003, the Commission established a task force on the Wider Europe under the authority of Guenter Verheugen, the Commissioner for Enlargement. Its job was to prepare policy recommendations for the region.

Apart from including the eastern and southern neighbours in a single policy statement, another odd aspect of the Communication was that it left out three countries that were already linked to the EU through PCAs and were already members of the Council of Europe and the Organisation for Security and Cooperation in Europe (OSCE), namely Georgia, Azerbaijan and Armenia. It explained that 'given their location' they 'also fall outside the scope of this initiative for the time being'. It thus emerged that the new initiative only referred to countries which 'do not currently have the perspective of membership of the EU'. In this way Albania was in a different category to the Ukraine, which was in a group containing Libya and Syria.

If one is looking for a stable circle of friends, one should be prudent with such forms of categorisation, especially if they serve to discourage the forces for reform in countries which already have PCAs with the EU. Georgia, alongside Azerbaijan and Armenia, faces a desperate economic situation with a very weak state structure, high levels of corruption as well as unresolved internal ethnic problems following military confrontations in the early 1990s. Prospects for these countries' EU accession are distant but they are in the Council of Europe. For these reasons, the Georgians see being left out of the Wider Europe initiative as a discouraging signal, especially as they have begun a process of approximating their laws with the EU. In the medium term, this region's only chance is to diversify its economic relations and clarify its internal situation. It needs cooperation with Russia and the inspiration of the possibility of eventual EU membership.

It is often said that there should be no new iron curtain to the east of the enlarged Union. But as the new member states advance towards western standards of social, political and cultural life, an asymmetry between them and the Ukraine, Belarus and Moldova seems likely to emerge. Because the new EU members have to adopt the Schengen *acquis*, they have begun tightening their borders to the east, in advance of accession. Obstructions to human and economic exchanges could easily develop. Rather than attempting a differentiated policy for every country from Morocco to Belarus, the EU should direct a more specific eastern neighbours policy or an eastern SAP in order to mitigate the difficulties for Ukraine, Belarus and Moldova resulting from enlargement and to counter the fear of isolation.

Economic cooperation with Belarus would advance the prospect for eventual political reform, while the policy of isolating Belarus merely shores up the Lukashenko regime. The EU should press for reform, making it clear that the country is considered part of the EU's neighbourhood. As the lack of democracy in Belarus does not cause political instability, the country gets less attention than it deserves from governments, whilst on a parliamentary level the European Parliament, in cooperation with the Council of Europe and OSCE parliamentary assemblies, has been prepared to keep open lines of communication.

Spokesmen for the Ukraine have echoed the concern that 'neighbourhood' is really a polite term for exclusion. The country considers that the model for steps beyond the PCA should be an association agreement on the lines with those agreed with the CEECs. Ukraine has suggested partial access to EU pre-accession programmes such as PHARE, ISPA and SAPARD. The current approach by the Commission might well achieve the opposite of what it aims to discourage: it could lead to a new, artificial division of Europe. Whatever its political weaknesses and internal divisions, it is clear that Ukraine's policy of European integration is the subject of wide domestic support and this perspective should not be closed by the EU.

Poland has called for a fully fledged 'eastern dimension' to EU policy to cover relations with Russia, Ukraine, Belarus and Moldova and at the same time strengthen EU policy towards the countries of the Caucasus and central Asia. As an example of the contribution which the new member states can make, Polish institutions, experts and non-governmental organisations offer experience of the transformation process. Poland has also recommended strengthened cooperation between the EU and the new neighbours in the area of justice and home affairs in order to face common problems such as organised crime, drug production, money-laundering and human-trafficking. EU assistance should go especially to strengthening the judiciary and the fight against corruption. Poland was also in favour of EU involvement to resolve the Transdniestra conflict in Moldova.

Russia

Developing a policy for EU relations with Russia should be more straight-forward because the world's largest country does not see itself as a future EU member. Russia does not need the EU for reassurance with regard to its destiny and identity. Its membership of the WTO is likely to lead to its consolidation as the leading market and principal investor in Ukraine, Belarus and Moldova. The EU needs to discuss neighbourhood issues with Russia, seek its support in bringing Belarus out of isolation and contribute to a solution to the Transdniestra conflict. But Russia has not yet been forthcoming in these matters and it has not been sensitive to the complaints of the EU (and the Council of Europe) about Russia's attempts to resolve the Chechnya problem through violent repressive measures.

Russia does not oppose EU integration or enlargement. It has an interest in peace and prosperity in its neighbourhood. The EU is already its main trading partner and a vital source of foreign direct investment. The future of the relationship depends primarily on how Russia evolves. After enlargement, consideration could be given to putting the EU–Russia relationship on a new basis. A report presented in October 2002 in Moscow by the Committee for 'Russia in a United Europe' (bringing together academics and politicians from Russia and the EU) proposed an agreement on establishing a special association between the Russian Federation and the EU. Without implying any Russian aspiration to join the EU, it would enable the partners to work together for sustainable economic development and cooperation in security matters whilst promoting the further development of democracy in Russia.

Russia will be profoundly affected by the widening and deepening processes of the EU, and the way in which the enlarged EU approaches Russia will influence these processes. A successful EU–Russia partnership would be a vital contribution to regional security. The anomalous situations in Georgia and Azerbaijan cannot continue forever and a solution to the problems of Abkhazia, South Ossetia and Nagorny Karabakh will be a test of Russia's readiness to contribute to regional security. Similarly the development of the EU's northern dimension should also address, in partnership with Russia, the problems of trade, pollution, organised crime and infrastructure development around the Baltic Sea. It will be interesting to see how the new member states influence EU–Russia relations. Whilst their sense of vulnerability will be reduced by NATO membership they are likely to want greater support for Ukraine and Georgia while countering Russian attempts to strengthen its influence on its 'near abroad'. On the other hand they will support EU cooperation with Russia as a way to secure energy supplies. They have a different perspective on transatlantic relations than some of the EU's founding members; it is possible that differences could also emerge on the future of EU–Russia relations.

In the introduction to his book *Europe – A History,* Norman Davies (p. 10) states that 'for more than 500 years the cardinal problem in defining Europe has centred on the inclusion or exclusion of Russia'. How the EU develops its relations with Russia will be just as important as how it deals with Turkey, and these issues will be at the forefront of discussion in the enlarged EU.

Other candidate countries?

A 'ring of friends' policy cannot ignore the fact that Switzerland, Iceland and Norway are civilised, peaceful, democratic, European countries. They represent what has been described as the 'forgotten enlargement' (Wallis 2002). Switzerland, which joined the UN only in 2002, did apply to join the EU in 1992 a few months before its people voted against joining the EEA, which resulted in its application being shelved. Norway has twice applied for membership, but its people have twice voted (in 1972 and 1994) against it. The three EEA states (Iceland, Norway and Liechtenstein) had to agree in 2003 to increase by 600 million euro their financial contribution to the alleviation of social and economic disparities in the ten new member states and in Portugal. Norway has had to pay a further 567 million euro in a bilateral agreement. They have to accept the EU's strategic decisions, over which they have no control, apart from some consultative opportunities on the specific issue of single market legislation. The EU should send a message of encouragement to Norway and Iceland that their applications for membership would be welcome. With their experience as stable democracies, and their ability to contribute to EU resources, they are the kind of neighbours that the EU should integrate. This contrasts, for example, with the treatment of Turkey, which participated in the Convention on the Future of Europe in 2002–3.

In its draft constitutional treaty the Convention in June 2003 proposed a specific article (Title VIII Article 1–56) dealing with the Union and its immediate environment. It provided for a loose but coherent framework bringing together existing arrangements with individual countries or groups of countries, giving for the first time recognition in the Treaty to the goal of strengthening the Union's wider European context. Whilst some Convention members had questioned the need for such an article and some suggested mentioning the Council of Europe and other relevant international organisations, others proposed adding a reference to the need for relations to be governed by basic principles such as democracy, the rule of law and human rights.

The draft treaty also included a proposal for a common EU system of border controls, including provisions to share the cost of managing the EU's external frontiers. The Baltic countries have led the voices in the enlarging Union who wish to have this particular burden shared as part of the EU's common policies in the field of justice and home affairs. It is natural that the geographical location of each member state gives it a particular perspective. Moreover the seriousness with which neighbouring countries cooperate with the EU in tackling issues related to crime and illegal immigration is a test of their willingness to contribute to Europe's security.

Conclusion

The continued attractiveness of the EU to so many of its neighbours confirms that the process of integration begun by six countries in the early 1950s is a powerful magnet and source of inspiration. For many of the EU's neighbours, it is something of a wonder to observe democratic countries sharing sovereignty and acting together to advance their common interest, without conflict or conquest. The nature and future borders of Europe are not just a matter for intellectual elites. All citizens, inside and outside the EU, are concerned by them. By its nature and timing, the Convention illustrated the intertwining of the processes of deepening and widening the Union. The debate on the future of the Union's borders is set to continue.

References

Davies, N. (1996) *Europe – A History*, Oxford: Oxford University Press.

Emerson, M. and Tocci, N. (2003) *The Rubik Cube of the Wider Middle East*, Brussels: Centre for European Policy Studies.

European Commission (2003) 'Wider Europe – Neighbourhood', COM (2003)104, Brussels.

European Commission (2003) 'The Stabilization and Association Process (SAP): Second Annual Reports', COM (2003)139, Brussels.

Mazower, M. (2000) *The Balkans*, London: Phoenix.

Wallis, D. (2002) *Forgotten Enlargement*, London: Centre for Reform.

White, S., McAllister, I. and Light, M. (2002) 'Enlargement and the new outsiders', *Journal of Common Market Studies*, Vol. 40, No. 1: 135–53.

Further reading

Cameron, F. (2003) *The Wider Europe*, Brussels: EPC Issue Paper One.

Emerson, M. (1998) *Redrawing the Map of Europe*, London: Macmillan.

Lewis, A. (ed.) (2002)*The EU and Ukraine: Neighbours, Friends, Partners?* London: Federal Trust.

Ronald, L. (ed.) (2000) *Norms and Nannies – The Impact of International Organisations in Central and East European States*, Lanham, MD: Rowman and Littlefield.

Sharpe, M.E. (1999) *Russia, the Caucasus and Central Asia*, New York: East-West Institute.

7   European security in flux

Antonio Missiroli and Gerrard Quille

Summary

The Iraq crisis revealed deep divisions between EU member states and between some member states and accession states, prompting some critics to dismiss the Union's attempts to create a genuine Common Foreign and Security Policy (CFSP). Yet CFSP has only been in existence for a decade and despite a poor start, due to the Balkans conflict, it has achieved some success. The EU now has common policies towards many regions, including the Balkans and the Middle East, is gradually developing a defence capability and started a number of operational peacekeeping missions in 2003. There was broad agreement in the Convention to strengthen the institutional structures of CFSP and to allow greater flexibility in defence arrangements. In the aftermath of the Iraq crisis, Mr Solana produced a security strategy paper that outlined potential threats to the Union and how the EU might best respond. This was a welcome first step for the EU in moving towards a common security doctrine. This chapter reviews the development of CFSP and European Security and Defence Policy (ESDP), assesses the EU's efforts to improve its military capabilities and examines the implications of enlargement on European security.

Introduction

The founding fathers of the EU always envisaged an eventual security role for the Union. Indeed, after the establishment of the ECSC in 1952, defence was the next item on the integration agenda. But it proved too sensitive an area and after the failure to set up a European Defence Community (EDC) in 1954, security and especially defence policy was not considered as part of the remit of the EU for a further four decades. Whilst European Political Cooperation (EPC) among the foreign ministries developed informally from 1970, then formally from 1987 in the SEA, the term 'security' was still only used in relation to its economic implications. Defence functions were thought to fall firmly within the remit of the Atlantic alliance and/or national governments.

The Maastricht Treaty established the CFSP that in principle included 'the eventual framing of a common defence policy', which could 'in time lead to a common defence'. In order to 'elaborate and implement decisions and actions with defence implications' however, the Union was to request another organisation, the Western European Union (WEU), to act. The WEU was created in 1954 out of the 1947 Brussels Treaty and included those EU members that were also NATO allies. The WEU was thus seen as 'an integral part' of the development of the Union. In June 1992, shortly after the signature of the Maastricht Treaty, the foreign and defence ministers of the WEU countries met at the Petersberg Hotel, near Bonn in Germany. They released a common declaration prioritising a new set of missions, distinct from traditional territorial defence, that became known as the 'Petersberg tasks' and were described as 'humanitarian and rescue tasks, peacekeeping tasks, and tasks of combat forces in crisis management, including peacemaking'. These were fine aims but many observers asked 'Where was the beef?'

The treaty review that was completed in Amsterdam in 1997 brought some important changes to CFSP. The position of High Representative was created and the 'Petersberg tasks' were incorporated into the TEU. Defence policy proper, however, remained off the immediate agenda of the Union. The Amsterdam Treaty review took place just four years after the start of CFSP in the most difficult of circumstances. The Balkan conflict posed an insuperable problem to resolve by diplomatic or economic pressure alone. To many Europeans, the EU had failed its first major test. At the same time, the CFSP made steady if unspectacular progress in a number of other areas. It helped resolve border and minority issues in central Europe under the first Stability Pact (also known as the Balladur Pact), it administered the war-torn city of Mostar in Yugoslavia (1994–6), it lobbied third countries successfully to secure the signing of several arms control treaties and, overall, it helped develop a culture of foreign and security policy cooperation between the member states. Without a military arm to back up its diplomacy, however, the limits of CFSP were obvious.

What changed the attitudes of member states was the dismal military performance of Europe in the 1998–9 Kosovo crisis. US planes flew 90 per cent of the bombing missions that were designed to force the Serbs out of Kosovo. As a result, the EU's two most important military powers, Britain and France, issued a declaration in St Malo in December 1998 that for the first time called on the EU to develop 'the capacity for autonomous action, backed up by credible military forces, the means to decide to use them, and a readiness to do so, in order to respond to international crises'. According to the declaration, such a commitment would not put into question either NATO or other national defence arrangements because the Union would take military action 'where the Alliance as a whole is not engaged' and 'without unnecessary duplication'. Still, the U-turn was remarkable.

In June 1999, at the Cologne European Council immediately after the Kosovo war, the Union as a whole embraced the St Malo 'spirit' and incorporated its wording in a common declaration. Here the terms 'conflict prevention' and 'crisis management' were first articulated in official EU documents linked to the 'Petersberg tasks' and marked the prospect of the EU taking over the tasks previously ascribed to the WEU, which in turn was considered as having 'completed' its function. ESDP was thus launched as part of CFSP. Six months later, the Helsinki European Council of December 1999 would set the headline goal of a rapid reaction force (RRF) and decide the establishment of the new EU bodies designed to manage ESDP. It was remarkable that all member states signed up for the ESDP, including the traditionally neutral and non-aligned countries (Sweden, Finland, Ireland, Austria). Indeed, Sweden and Finland were the twin driving forces behind this initiative.

The development of ESDP

The present momentum behind ESDP derives largely from these recent and sudden developments. The member states did not dwell much further on where the Union's own strategic priorities of action might lie or on what kind of tasks the Union might need to think about carrying out 'where the Alliance as a whole is not engaged'. Instead their attention focused on 'means' and in four areas in particular.

New institutions

First, the EU was active as regards institution-building. New political and military bodies were set up in Brussels. The Political and Security Committee (PSC) was to provide overall political and strategic guidance. It was in turn served by the EU Military Committee (EUMC), composed of the chiefs of staff of the 15, supported by a 70-strong EU Military Staff (EUMS). Gradually the PSC developed into an important policy-making body, causing some jealousies with Coreper.

Helsinki headline goal

Second, the 1999 Helsinki European Council initiated the much cited Helsinki Headline Goal (HHG) process and a new debate, alongside a much older one in NATO, on European defence capabilities, which has been a mainstay of subsequent EU summit meetings and expert debate. The HHG consists of a corps-sized force of 50–60,000 men, with appropriate air and naval support, deployable in two months and sustainable for at least one year. (At the Feira European Council, June 2000, it was decided to set a civilian headline goal consisting of a contingent of 5,000 policemen deployable in two months and sustainable for at least one year.)

Initially it was easy for member states to volunteer enough quantities of manpower and assets. At the capability commitments conference in November 2000, they were able to draw upon Europe's formally vast but mostly inefficient military resources to satisfy the member states' initial operational target (Clarke *et al.* 2001).

Capabilities

It soon became clear, however, that there were serious gaps in the EU's military capabilities. Two reports by the EUMS, reviewing all European military capabilities and member states' commitments, revealed significant shortfalls in 42 areas. At the second commitments conference on 19 November 2001, a third catalogue was produced, under which the short-falls were documented and monitored for improvement. By May 2003 the HHG were considered as met by the Union, even though considerable shortfalls still remained in the domain of strategic military capabilities. Progress on the shortfalls is carried out by the member states under the so-called European capability action plan (ECAP).

EU–NATO

Fourth, whilst the process for dealing with institutional and capability shortfalls was quickly codified in the Union's machinery, the process for putting military forces in the field was held up by the need to seek an agreement, known as 'Berlin Plus', on access to NATO assets. The agreement, initially conceived for WEU proper, then handed over directly to the EU, had been blocked for three years, alternately by Turkey or Greece. The breakthrough came in December 2002 and was finalised with the general security agreement in March 2003, in the wake of the radical political change that had occurred in Turkey the month before (Missiroli 2002, 2003d). As a result, the Union gained access to NATO planning capabilities and can now work on the assumption that it has access to the NATO capabilities it requires, even when the formal decision to do so will be taken on a case-by-case basis. However partial, the deal has somewhat 'freed' ESDP of an important constraint and it has made the 'devolution' of some NATO tasks and operations to the EU possible.

These developments have been generally well received, but a lack of linkage between the main policy threads means that questions remain about the commitment of member states to seeing through what they have started. Some have called for an EU strategic concept to meet this require-ment and to establish a balance with the present 'bottom up' process and provide direction for the long-term needs and planning of the Union. Understanding the strategic rationale and 'vision' of the Union remained mostly an academic pursuit until recently, when the ESDP received significant attention in four key developments.

European Convention

The draft constitutional treaty made some interesting proposals on CFSP/ESDP. It proposed the creation of an EU foreign minister to facilitate coherence and coordination between EU institutions and bureaucracies. By contrast, the new draft articles on decision-making still display all the roadblocks, especially the retention of unanimity, that have long slowed down or impaired CFSP. At the same time, the scope of the original 'Petersberg tasks' is significantly broadened in that it also encompasses 'joint disarmament operations, . . . military and advice assistance tasks, . . . conflict prevention . . . and post-conflict stabilization'.

Furthermore, the new articles entail as many as five potentially different formats and scenarios for closer cooperation in the ESDP domain, that is, for policy arrangements including only some, but not all member states. For example, they refer to an internal solidarity clause, armaments cooperation and procurement, 'structured cooperation' based on 'high military capability criteria', mutual defence proper, and, finally, the implementation of certain tasks by a group of willing and able member states. Some of these formats are entirely open, some do not look like that, some are to be launched consensually, some are not; and some are relatively undetermined. On the one hand, this creates confusion. On the other, it keeps the door open to various, even competing developments, thus enabling rather than binding the Union's action in the future.

One of the drawbacks of the draft treaty was the limited involvement of the EP in overseeing the development of CFSP/ESDP. Given the strong public interest in the development of an EU security policy it would be preferable for the EP to play a stronger role in overseeing EU actions in this sensitive field. On the whole, the draft constitutional treaty, if adopted without significant modifications, would appear to make CFSP marginally more coherent and focused, while substantially widening the scope and the modalities for the implementation of ESDP.

Solana's European security strategy (ESS) paper

In June 2003, Javier Solana issued a security strategy paper, entitled *A Secure Europe in a Better World* (http://ue.eu.int/pressdata/EN/reports/76255.pdf) that set the new general parameters for future common external action. This long-awaited step gives the Union a much broader assessment than previously of the potential threats to European security (including the proliferation of weapons of mass destruction and international terrorism) and of the Union's responsibilities in the world. Whilst the issue of an EU security strategy has been on the agenda for many years, the timing of the Solana paper was partly a European response to the post 9/11 security priorities of the US and partly an exercise in healing divisions within Europe over Iraq. What remains to be seen is whether the document will sufficiently capture the imagination of the member states for them to provide the political will necessary to transform Solana's comprehensive strategy into a coherent European approach to meeting contemporary security problems (Quille 2003; Cameron 2003).

In the paper, Solana stresses that the Union needs 'to develop a strategic culture that fosters early, rapid and, when necessary, robust intervention'. At the same time, the added value of the EU as a security actor, not just regionally but also globally, is reaffirmed, although 'extending the zone of security around Europe' remains a top priority. The ESS stresses the Union's unique capacity to mobilise a wide array of policy tools well beyond the military. It argues that the Union, in cooperation with its international partners and within the framework of the UN Charter, should play an active role in order to strengthen the international order and promote the rule of law and good governance.

The Solana paper is a broad document that highlights European strengths and values in pursuing security priorities. Whilst these priorities in themselves meet some US security concerns, they do not amount to a European endorsement of US methods. The strategy thus provides a framework within which traditional EU priorities (conflict prevention, poverty and governance within regional dialogue) are balanced with the new priorities of the member states in responding to WMD, non-proliferation and international terrorism. It will of course be crucial to see whether the new priorities lead to a reduction in commitment to existing ones.

Armaments

Compared to the US, the EU does not get enough 'bang for its buck' (or euro) in defence procurement. After many years of hesitation, the member states, the European Commission, the presidency and defence industry are collectively pushing for a breakthrough at the EU level on armaments policy. The argument is that if defence spending is not to increase, one obvious way of bridging capability gaps is through increased armaments cooperation. Joint procurement of the necessary equipment would offer savings through economies of scale and reduced duplication. However, this might not be such an easy option to achieve: despite much rhetoric about the need for greater armaments cooperation within the EU, actual results are so far disappointing. European defence industrial consolidation is still patchy and defence procurement remains oriented towards national needs (see Table 7.1). Two dominant features are evident in the defence industrial scene: a growing monopolisation in the aerospace and defence electronics sectors; and a lack of consolidation of mostly subsidised, and protected, national capacities in the other sectors.

Table 7.1 Defence spending in R&D and equipment

Country	Total expenditure	Research & development	Equipment procurement
Austria	1,625	11	339
Belgium	2,607	1	254
Denmark	2,478	1	361
Finland	1,648	–	536
France	28,813	3,313	5,770
Germany	24,826	1,410	3,704
Greece	3,469	26	1,466
Netherlands	6,564	72	1,486
Ireland	772	0	51
Italy	17,046	35	2,470
Luxembourg	107	0	7
Portugal	1,654	4	403
Spain	7,445	190	1,156
Sweden	4,781	113	2,365
UK	36,793	4,371	9,266
Total	140,628	9,547	29,634
Average	9,375.2	636.5	1,975.6

Source: International Institute for Strategic Studies 2000–2001; all figures given in euro millions.

Beyond 'Berlin Plus'

Now that the series of agreements that constitute 'Berlin Plus' are in place, the two organisations can more systematically engage with one another. Although this has fostered more formal inter-institutional exchanges, mainly on capabilities and operations, it has also highlighted an underlying tension between them. For instance, the need for the EU to have its own advanced planning capability, such as NATO has at SHAPE, was thought to be redundant now that the Union has recourse to such assets under Berlin Plus. However, the Union's interest in places such as central Africa highlighted a very interesting question: who at NATO would have the plans for such an operation? When the EU launched its operation in the Congo in the summer of 2003, concern was expressed that NATO was not formally part of the process. Shortly afterwards, at the NATO ministerial in Madrid, the previously warmly held idea of the EU taking over from NATO in Bosnia from 2004 was put back until an internal review at NATO had taken place.

Structural problems

Despite the dependency on member states' political will and the inherent complexity of EU crisis management and defence developments, significant obstacles remain in achieving an effective ESDP. These structural aspects of European defence have dogged the member states for some years, at both the national and NATO level, in that they are seen as individually incapable of producing the necessary military means to meet their security ambitions. Although it was relatively easy to commit nominal national capabilities to the RRF and submit national equipment to the HHG, governments across the EU are realising how difficult it is to move from identifying gaps to committing resources to make up the shortfalls. This should not have been so much of a surprise given the difficulties encountered by NATO and its defence capabilities initiative since 1999.

Financing ESDP

Putting up the necessary military means for crisis management, that is mobilising the resources that are essential to meet the EU's own expectations and ambitions, is likely to become the crucial issue for the ESDP in the future. Unlike a few years ago, the political willingness to act together as Europeans is now there, at least in principle. Although largely untested, the basic structures for action are there too (Rutten 2001). Both, however, must rely on adequate means and financial support. In this sense, key concerns are European overall spending trends, functional spending within current budgets and security 'burden sharing' (Missiroli 2003a,b,c).

European defence spending began to stabilise around the mid-1990s after a period of decline in the immediate aftermath of the Cold War and most commentators believe that the present level is likely to remain stable for the foreseeable future (see Table 7.2). Members of the EU's Stability and Growth Pact are under strong pressure not to expand public expenditure, due both to the EU's self-imposed financial discipline and low rates of growth. This will have an impact upon defence budgets as well as other areas of public spending. Nevertheless, the US has been putting enormous pressure on Europe, especially since 9/11, to increase defence spending and address the so-called 'capabilities gap' (Jost 2000). Needless to say, the gap (and/or the perception thereof) has further deepened since Operation 'Enduring Freedom' in Afghanistan and the dramatic boost to defence expenditure in the US. In terms of raw military power, the US is now not just in a class of its own but is approaching the point where it will spend as much as the rest of the world put together. In Europe, however, current plans indicate that defence spending within the Union overall will not increase substantially in real terms (although there are signs to the contrary in France). Nor would an increase in spending necessarily provide more military capability, unless accompanied by reform of inefficient procurement processes, ministerial bureaucracies, and relevant industrial sectors (Quille *et al.* 2003) (see Figure 7.1).

Having different perceptions, concepts, objectives and a different geography, it is almost natural that Europe spends less than America on defence, roughly half as much in 2003, and has different budgetary priorities. There is also the legacy of the Cold War to consider. For several decades,

Table 7.2 EU defence spending trends

Defence expenditure (constant 2000 US$)

Year	US$m			US$per capita			% GDP			No. armed forces (000)	
	1985	2000	2001	1985	2000	2001	1985	2000	2001	1985	2001
Austria	1,952	1,612	1,471	258	200	182	1.2	0.9	0.8	54.7	34.6
Belgium	6,223	3,212	3,017	631	313	293	3.0	1.4	1.3	91.6	39.4
Denmark	3,161	2,395	2,409	618	453	454	2.2	1.5	1.5	29.6	21.4
Finland	2,271	1,560	1,432	463	301	275	2.8	1.3	1.2	36.5	32.3
France	49,378	34,053	32,909	895	575	553	4.0	2.6	2.6	464.3	273.7
Germany	53,303	27,924	26,902	702	341	328	3.2	1.5	1.5	478.0	308.4
Greece	3,521	5,528	5,517	354	523	520	7.0	4.9	4.8	201.5	159.2
Netherlands	8,991	6,027	6,257	621	381	394	3.1	1.6	1.7	105.5	50.4
Ireland	484	629	623	136	167	164	1.8	0.6	0.5	13.7	10.5
Italy	25,974	22,488	20,966	455	391	365	2.3	2.1	2.0	385.1	230.4
Luxembourg	96	129	145	263	299	332	0.9	0.7	0.8	0.7	0.9
Portugal	1,853	2,221	2,226	181	223	223	3.1	2.1	2.0	73.0	43.6
Spain	11,390	7,063	6,938	295	178	174	2.4	1.2	1.2	320.0	143.5
Sweden	4,826	4,610	3,898	578	524	443	3.3	2.0	1.9	65.7	33.9
UK	48,196	35,655	34,714	852	601	583	5.2	2.5	2.5	334.0	211.4
Total EU	221,619	155,106	149,424							2,655	1,594
EU average	14,775	10,340	9,962	487	365	352	3.0	1.8	1.75	177	106

Source: IISS, Military Balance 2002–3.

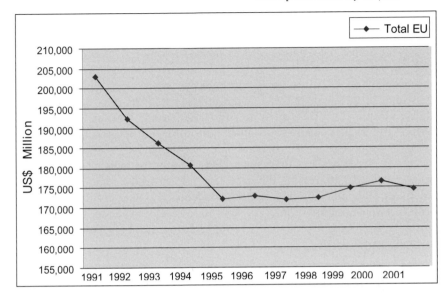

Figure 7.1 EU defence spending trends.

Europeans relied entirely on the Americans for the essence of their collective defence, thus leaving to them key command-and-control and strategic capabilities while providing manpower (mainly conscripts) and land-based assets that are of little use now. The constant and unflattering comparisons with the massive American defence effort set standards for the European effort that are impossible to meet, thereby engendering a sense of frustration and futility. Europeans should rather set objectives for the level of defence capability based upon their own strategic priorities and not upon comparison and competition with the US (see Table 7.3).

A discussion focused exclusively on national defence budgets is too narrow in scope and, above all, inadequate to tackle the real needs and

Table 7.3 Total EU and US defence spending

	1991	1992	1993	1994	1995	1996
Total EU	202,884	192,412	186,276	180,735	172,265	172,882
USA	335,473	354,507	335,940	316,776	298,376	282,231

	1997	1998	1999	2001	2002
Total EU	171,944	172,549	174,954	176,560	174,596
USA	280,785	274,278	275,057	285,679	281,426

Source: SIPRI 2002, all figures given in constant US dollar millions.

shortcomings of an effective EU crisis management capability. In fact, 'burden-sharing' is not just about comparing the budgets of the ministries of defence across the Atlantic or even inside the Union. Defence budgets, in turn, do not cover only the defence 'function' and expenditure on defence and security as a means for comprehensive crisis management may lie elsewhere in national budgets. Some military budgets may look quantitatively adequate, yet they often do so for the 'wrong' reasons. The cases of Greece and Turkey, who spend more than other European allies per head to match each other's force structures in the Aegean Sea, abundantly prove this point. Yet it is a fact that, since 1990, Europeans have all reaped their peace dividends, addressing the necessary reform of the military only late, reactively and, more often than not, inadequately. As a result, in Europe only Britain maintains a level of national defence expenditure that even rivals the US in per capita and per soldier terms, and only France is trying to catch up.

Security 'burden-sharing'

Traditional 'burden-sharing' debates within NATO have focused upon the fact that the US contributed overwhelmingly more in defence terms to the security of western Europe during the Cold War. Today such 'burden-sharing' debates take place within the context of an evolving CFSP and a broader understanding of security that includes EU enlargement, climate change and aid to the third world. In this broader context EU contributions to international security are no longer pale reflections of US contributions, in fact, quite the reverse. For instance, European countries contribute three times as much as the US to development aid and will soon pay almost twice as much into the relevant UN budget.

Paradoxically, at approximately 50 per cent of the US total, European expenditure on defence makes for the second largest in the world, well ahead of Russia in third place. Thus, the overall amount of public money devoted to defence, to which one should add the sizeable funds that the member states and the EU devote to security at large, including conflict prevention and post-conflict rehabilitation, could well meet the stated goals of the Union's foreign and security policy. Put together, the EU-15 bear the main military burden of peacekeeping operations in the Balkans and largely finance peace-building in the region. They are also responsible for the lion's share of civilian aid in the Middle East as well as of post-conflict reconstruction in Afghanistan.

There is, however, no room for complacency. The EU-15 have a defence budget problem, starting with the strong imbalance between personnel and equipment expenditure that affects almost all members, and ending with the small amount (one-quarter of the US total) that they spend on R&D. The main problem lies with the quality of European defence spending, i.e.

with the way in which EU member states allocate their limited resources. Defence procurement is fragmented and nationally focused, thus dispersing financial means that could be better used for the common good without duplicating assets. The existing cooperative programmes such as Euro-fighter, Meteor or A400M, are all *ad hoc* and purely intergovernmental, creating extra costs and delays. The overall level of investment is largely insufficient if measured against the shortfalls that the member states have agreed to address together. Uneven spending across EU countries, even among the main spenders, further creates a potential 'burden-sharing' problem inside the Union. Neither do the EU-15 use comparable budgetary invoicing or have compatible procurement cycles, which further complicates policy coordination and convergence.

Any solution, therefore, should address both quantitative and qualitative problems and, arguably, should do so at the same time and within the same policy framework. Even if it was possible and accepted, simply spending more would not necessarily generate the required capabilities, since 'pork barrel' politics is well established in the defence field. Even if spending better were to take precedence, however, spending more would become all the more necessary: savings are certainly possible in the short term, but reconfiguring expenditure will in itself require an investment of time and money (in terms of early retirement schemes for redundant personnel, base closures etc.); while increasing capabilities will mean buying or leasing new equipment off the shelf.

A further problem is that member states still do not all share the same views on the scope of the 'Petersberg tasks'. There is certainly a broad consensus over their so-called 'low end', for which most of the necessary resources, including those related to non-military crisis management, are already available both across the Union (member states) and in Brussels: the Commission's rapid reaction mechanism; the EC humanitarian office (ECHO); Europe-aid, plus the Council secretariat. By contrast, 'high end' missions are more controversial and their understanding seems differently nuanced even among the main military players in the EU. Differences do not necessarily lie in the amount of military force involved on the ground, although air power varies significantly, but rather in the description and mandate of the envisaged mission, including the desirability of NATO (read US) involvement.

Such differences represent an important part of the reality of EU crisis management, whereby the member states' forces cannot be considered a single unit, unlike the American ones. There are certainly unnecessary duplic-ations and it might be necessary to aim at some unavoidable duplications of capabilities *vis-à-vis* the US (especially as far as strategic assets are con-cerned) (Schake 2002). Yet it is still barely conceivable that EU members (smaller ones included) should give up their entire armed services and functions that are considered part of the constitutional tasks of the state.

ESDP in action

Despite all these obstacles and limits, ESDP has evolved considerably in a short time. Since January 2003, it has been engaged in three missions: in Bosnia-Herzegovina; the Former Yugoslav Republic of Macedonia and the Democratic Republic of Congo. These missions have performed a variety of tasks, from law enforcement and ceasefire monitoring to security and humanitarian crisis management. On the whole, over 2,000 police and military personnel have been involved in these missions. Military operations are important test cases for the Union's ability to apply some of the security policy instruments it envisaged under the Helsinki and Feira headline goals. Although limited in scope and time, the 2003 engagements are the first hands-on manifestation of the EU's security and defence dimension, which may lead to more ambitious interventions within and beyond its immediate periphery.

EUPM (Bosnia and Herzegovina)

Launched on 1 January 2003, the European Union Police Mission (EUPM) in Bosnia-Herzegovina represents the EU's first-ever civilian crisis management operation under ESDP. It is based on a Council decision of 11 March 2002, following the United Nations Security Council's (UNSC) endorsement (Resolution 1396 of 5 March 2002) for an EU engagement. On 4 October 2002, the EU signed an agreement with the Bosnian authorities that defined the conditions and terms of the EUPM. Taking over from the UN's International Police Task Force (IPTF), which had been in place since December 1995, the operation seeks to establish local law enforcement capabilities that can contribute to the stability of the region. Some 531 police officers, about 80 per cent from EU member states and 20 per cent from third states, perform monitoring, mentoring and inspection activities.

The EUPM has a mandate for three years (until 31 December 2005) and an annual budget of 38 million euro, of which 20 million euro are financed from the EU budget. The police officers are backed by some 400 support staff. The EUPM, whose headquarters are located in Sarajevo, is divided into three departments, namely operations, planning and development, plus administration and support services. A Danish officer, Sven Frederiksen, was appointed police commissioner for the operation: he works in close contact with Lord Ashdown, the EU special representative (and UN envoy) in the country.

'Concordia' (Former Yugoslav Republic of Macedonia)

On 31 March 2003, the EU launched the 'Concordia' mission in the Former Yugoslav Republic of Macedonia (FYROM), its first-ever military operation. EU forces took over NATO's Operation 'Allied Harmony' with the aim of contributing further to a stable, secure environment in Macedonia and ensuring the implementation of the August 2001 Ohrid framework agreement, which settled the conflict between Macedonian Slavs and Albanians. The EU force, within which France acts as 'framework' nation, patrols the ethnic Albanian-populated regions of Macedonia that border Albania, Serbia and Kosovo.

The operation, requested by the FYROM and endorsed by UNSC resolution 1371, contains personnel from 13 EU member states (all except Ireland and Denmark) and 14 non-member states. The total forces are a modest 350 lightly armed military personnel and the budget for the first six months of the operation was 6.2 million euro. While 'Concordia' constitutes an EU-led mission, the Union draws on NATO assets and capabilities under the 'Berlin Plus' arrangement. The EU's operation in FYROM, therefore, also represents the first test case for the strategic EU–NATO partnership for crisis management, embodied in the agreement of December 2002.

'Artemis' (Democratic Republic of Congo)

With the aim of preventing a large-scale humanitarian and civil crisis in Ituri, a region in the north-east of the Democratic Republic of Congo, the EU responded to an appeal by the UN Secretary General and launched a military operation on 12 June 2003. In accordance with the mandate set out in UNSC resolution 1484 (30 May 2003), the French-led 'Artemis' mission seeks to contribute to the stabilisation of security conditions and the improvement of the humanitarian situation in Bunia, the Ituri capital. The multinational force is mandated to protect camps of internally displaced persons and secure Bunia airport, as well as ensure the safety of the civilian population, UN personnel and the wider humanitarian presence. The force has about 1,800 soldiers, mostly French. 'Artemis' is the EU's first military operation outside Europe and, unlike the other two missions, does not rely on NATO assistance.

These two military operations (Missiroli 2003c) highlight the willingness of the EU to take concrete action in crisis management tasks. Importantly, the second operation, 'Artemis', reveals that the 'framework nation' concept, initially elaborated within the WEU, can be useful for achieving some semblance of 'rapidity' in response to a call for a EU multinational operation. This flexibility reflects the reality that certain member states have the necessary structures to take the lead in multinational operations and that in a Union of 25 it will not always be possible to include everyone in an operation, as was attempted with 'Concordia'.

Enlargement and CFSP/ESDP

The enlargement of the EU has been for decades, and still is, a quintessential security policy. By extending the Union's norms, rules, opportunities and constraints to the applicants, it has made, and will make, instability and conflict in the wider region much less likely. It is also a security policy in its own right because the entrants have brought, and will bring in, interests and skills that broaden the scope of the common external policies.

But the current enlargement is unlike previous ones in size and scope. How will a 25-member EU stretching from Estonia to Portugal, from Sweden to Cyprus, be able to define its strategic interests? To what extent will this affect the way in which the EU projects itself externally? How will enlargement affect the functioning of CFSP/ESDP? What will be the attitude of third countries such as the US or Russia? In a Union of 25, alliances and coalitions may easily shift according to the contingencies and the issues at stake. What can be assessed at this stage, therefore, is only what priorities, preferences, general attitudes and specific interests the current applicant are likely to bring into the present EU-15 (Missiroli 2003b).

The tiny new Mediterranean member states, Cyprus and Malta, are likely to focus essentially on their immediate neighbourhood. For Cyprus, a solution to the division of the island is a top priority. Cyprus is also affected by any changes in the Greek–Turkish relationship. Both island states have neutrality enshrined in their constitution and would have difficulty participating in any major EU military operation.

For the CEECs, nuances still persist (due also to their different historical experience, geopolitical position, sheer size and available resources), but some discernible common features also seem to emerge. The CEECs had few problems with CFSP until the Iraq crisis blew up in early 2003. They then faced a difficult split within the EU and within the Atlantic alliance over supporting US/UK readiness to take military action against Saddam Hussein's regime. The CEECs' main concern was not to undermine NATO or the strategic ties with the US. Some of them were wary of ESDP suspecting that involvement in ESDP, might come as an alternative to future NATO membership or, worse, as a consolation prize for not being admitted into the Alliance, which had always been their main security policy goal (Cameron and Primatovera 2003).

Conversely, for those candidates who were already NATO members, the key issue was notably the establishment of a clearly defined relationship with the Alliance, whereby all relevant decisions would be taken at 15 + 6 (EU members plus other European allies). Furthermore, they hardly appreciated the initial EU approach, whereby they were simply included in the broader category of 'third countries', together with fellow non-allied candidates but especially countries like Russia or Ukraine. It was not until the spring of 2000 that a more differentiated approach prevailed within the EU, although that did not entirely dispel the lingering fears of the CEECs.

Over time, however, their attitudes have evolved towards a warmer acceptance of the ESDP, on condition that its implementation turns into a positive-sum, rather than a zero-sum, game between the EU and NATO.

The fear of potentially even higher hurdles to overcome on the road to accession prompted a more constructive attitude on the applicants' side. Some residual ambivalence over the implications of ESDP is still there, however, and may resurface in the presence of unexpected developments in the region and/or in transatlantic relations. A good example has been offered recently by the pressure that the US administration has put on them (and on some of the current member states) to sign separate bilateral deals with Washington, exempting American forces from the jurisdiction of the newly constituted International Criminal Court (ICC): a pressure that only Romania gave in to initially but others were tempted to follow suit, until the EU, in late September 2002, agreed on a set of guidelines to be adopted and respected by all present and future members in their negotiations with Washington.

The main issue for most acceding CEECs is that of participation on equal footing with the older member states, articulated as equality in decision-making and inclusiveness in policy implementation. This concern, related to their shifting from policy-takers to policy-makers, was also apparent in the Convention proceedings, and will probably become the criterion against which they will measure their support for ESDP within the EU framework.

Another important issue is the scope and outreach of CFSP/ESDP. For historical as well as geographical reasons, none of the countries under consideration has significant overseas interests or extensions, with the exception of sizeable, often vocal ethnic/national communities in the United States, let alone a colonial past. In contrast to previous enlargements, therefore, the forthcoming one will not entail a significant widening of the horizons of the Union's external policies, although the Poles especially and the Baltics intend to foster their 'special relationship' with the US.

All current applicants, however, have a strong interest in the formulation of those external policies of the enlarged Union that might affect their immediate vicinity. After all, most of them will become the new external frontier of the EU. The permeability and safety of the eastern borders and all common 'direct neighbourhood' policies will become vital interests and shape their behaviour on CFSP and other issues. The condition of national minorities, cross-border trade and visa regulations, energy and environmental issues, Balkan stability, relations with Belarus, Ukraine, Moldova and, of course, Russia will be priority issues. In this sense, the new members' impact on CFSP and ESDP will be geographically limited but intensely focused. Yet again, this may not necessarily mean that there will be a sort of central European 'bloc' on, say, relations with Russia (or Belarus).

As regards the US and NATO, the CEECs all pushed during the Convention for a clear understanding between the Alliance and the Union. Whether already NATO members or just future ones, they do not want to be forced to choose between Washington and Brussels on security matters. While their markedly 'Atlanticist' orientation, as abundantly proved also by opinion polls, will add next to nothing to the overall spectrum of existing positions among the current EU members, after accession it may slightly tip the internal balance of the Union in that direction. However, actual membership may change the perception of national interests and shape new loyalties.

The decision, adopted by the Alliance at its Prague summit in November 2002, to invite the seven central and east European countries still outside it to join NATO by May 2004 is likely to reinforce their 'NATO-first' approach, at least in the short term. Once in and the realities of membership became apparent, however, their attitude may shift towards a more balanced assessment of priorities and goals. In other words, there may not be a central and east European 'bloc' on CFSP/ESDP in general either, although it will be quite normal for them to try and prevent any competition between the Alliance and the Union. What is likely, at any rate, is that Bulgaria and Romania will try to make the most of their NATO-only membership (at least as long as that is the case), also as regards ESDP and its cooperation with the Alliance.

In spite of their relatively short record of freedom of action (and, for some, sheer independence) on the international scene, all the CEECs have, over the past few years, been increasingly engaged in peace support operations, mostly, but not exclusively, in the western Balkans. As a rule, they have done so as modular components of bigger multinational units and under foreign command. Much as the contributions have been limited in absolute numbers and restricted in their functions, they have nevertheless proved the willingness and ability of the applicants to participate and perform in peace support operations.

In most CEECs, participation in NATO-led or EU-led missions is seen as a driving factor towards some sort of role specialisation. Such specialisation is about making a virtue out of necessity: financial, technical and human resources are scarce and have to be channelled and focused on viable objectives. This is all the more important since all the countries under consideration are in the process of overhauling and modernising their military forces. Moreover, the ways in which, notably, the Czechs have focused on developing chemical weapon decontamination units, or the Romanians mountain light infantry, represent important success stories. In other words, functional role specialisation (military as well as civilian) is a path that could soon prove unavoidable, even for current EU members. The almost generalised creation of multinational units on a sub-regional basis seems to have become more substantial and less symbolic than before, along with the joint leasing or 'pooling' of certain capabilities (aircraft and logistics).

Similar constraints, and opportunities, apply to the acceding countries' defence procurement policy proper. While most countries are still substituting or upgrading old equipment from the Soviet era, the need to become more interoperable with NATO allies is putting additional pressure on public budgets and decision-makers. Procurement policy, however, remains largely driven by political considerations, taking increasingly into account the added value of domestic job creation in high-tech sectors that may prove crucial in the future (see Table 7.4). Much will depend on how the EU will respond to the increased US pressure, especially on the acceding EU and NATO countries, to 'buy American' and follow Washington's lead also on operational matters. Polish participation in the post-war military administration of Iraq raised eyebrows in several EU capitals.

Conclusion

The Iraq crisis highlighted, once more, the fragility of CFSP and the reality of divisions within Europe, but it also prompted the member states to respond by beginning the process of sketching an EU security strategy that meets some US concerns, while articulating a particular and coherent European approach. The short-term success of the Union's security policy will depend largely on the personal qualities of the first foreign minister in making the most of the institutional arrangements, whilst reassuring the 25 member states and a vigilant US. Although the evolving security policy framework provides for greater coherence with a distinct European character, the new institutional arrangements will take some time to become fully effective. This will limit the speed of further CFSP/ESDP developments, which may suit the new member states as they adjust to their new roles and begin to develop their own visions on the future of the Union.

Meanwhile, the Union will continue to implement existing policies and the three EU operations launched in 2003 represent a major breakthrough for ESDP. For the first time, the Union is proactively engaging in security affairs and covering a variety of tasks that stretch from policing to military intervention. The missions show that the EU is capable of reacting to ongoing or emerging humanitarian/security crises and able to contribute to peace enforcement, reconstruction and stabilisation.

Needless to say, this will be all the easier to achieve whenever and wherever there is no major disagreement with the Americans over the respective roles of NATO, the EU and other possible formats and/or coalitions. The current blossoming of ESDP, therefore, should help put the Iraq EU débâcle of spring 2003 in perspective, allowing the demanding European public to be slightly more optimistic about the scope of shared interests and polices under CFSP.

At the same time, it is important to recall that EU missions thus far remain very limited in scope and still depend heavily on the leadership, commitment and interest of major EU member states. Certain member states in particular may not always be keen on engaging their national assets and capabilities within a EU framework: it is happening with

Table 7.4 Accession states' defence spending in recent years

| | Defence expenditure | | | | | | | | | No. armed forces (000) | |
| | US$m | | | US$ per capita | | | % GDP | | | | |
Year	1985	2000	2001	1985	2000	2001	1985	2000	2001	1985	2001
Cyprus	132	361	315	198	414	350	3.6	4.1	3.6	10.0	10.0
Czech Republic	–	–	–	–	–	–	–	–	–	–	–
Estonia	n.a.	78	92	n.a.	55	66	n.a.	1.5	1.7	n.a.	4.5
Hungary	3,588	805	909	337	81	92	7.2	1.7	1.8	106.0	33.8
Latvia	n.a.	71	85	n.a.	29	35	n.a.	1.0	1.2	n.a.	6.5
Lithuania	n.a.	199	211	n.a.	54	57	n.a.	1.8	1.8	n.a.	12.2
Poland	8,706	3,092	3,408	234	80	88	8.1	2.0	2.0	319.0	206.0
Romania	2,109	940	969	93	42	43	4.5	2.6	2.5	189.5	103.0
Slovak Republic	–	342	386	–	–	–	–	1.7	1.9	–	26
Slovenia	–	273	277	–	137	139	–	1.5	1.5	–	7.6
Total accession '10'	14,535	7,101	6,652							624.5	206
Average for the '10'	1,454	710	665	86	89	87	2.3	1.8	1.8	63	21
EU '15' Average	14,775	10,340	9,962	487	365	352	3.0	1.8	1.75	177	106

Source: IISS, Military Balance 2002–3.

Notes:
Figures for the Slovak Republic are provided by SIPRI's 'Military Expenditure Database'. Figures are in US$ m at constant 2000 prices and exchange rates are for the calendar year. Figures in constant dollars are converted using the market exchange rate for all countries.

'Artemis', but it did not happen earlier in Ivory Coast or Sierra Leone, where France and Britain, respectively, preferred to act autonomously, applying the 'subsidiarity' principle to peace support. Other (especially new) member states may prefer to act militarily only or primarily within NATO and/or with the Americans. The fact is that the EU has no military capabilities at its own disposal. Moreover, significant command and control capability shortfalls among member states mean that any complex, high-end operation would have to depend on NATO support. True, 'Concordia' implemented the Berlin Plus agreement, yet the long-term relationship between the Union and NATO remains to be fully defined. Besides, EU operations thus far, while important symbolically, are not complex operationally. None of the current operations, with the exception of 'Artemis', pushes EU military capabilities and political will to the limit, but a new Balkan mission would be a problem. In this respect, the EU remains untested across the full spectrum of peace support missions.

This said, it is hardly questionable that EU, at long last, is now in the peacekeeping business. Much remains to be improved, tested, learned and fine-tuned. Yet the Union, whose current 15 member states also cover more than 40 per cent of the UN peacekeeping budget proper, can claim to have become a fully fledged actor in its own right also in this domain. The geographical and strategic scope of its action is still subject to significant evolution. For the time being, it encompasses the immediate proximity of the EU (the western Balkans, maybe Moldova) and, potentially, the wider cultural/historical/economic proximity represented by some post-colonial states in Africa (Congo) as well as further away (East Timor). It is not by accident that these areas are also the main recipients of EU direct aid and assistance schemes and that they are on the receiving end of preferential trade arrangements, although the Union is still far from linking up effectively all the policy tools at its disposal. The functional scope of EU security policy is likely to be varied, mixed in both space and time, and encompassing economic, civilian and also military components. Finally, the 'doctrine' and the policy 'style' are expected to stem more or less directly from the norms, principles and values that have hitherto inspired the very process of European integration.

References

Cameron, F. (2003) *An EU Strategic Concept*, Brussels: EPC Issue Paper no 5, June.

Cameron, F. and Primatovera, A. (2003) *The Convention, Enlargement and CFSP*, European Policy Institutes Network Working Paper, June.

Clarke, M., Garden, T. and Quille, G. (2001) *Making Sense of the Helsinki Headline Goal*, Discussion Paper, London: Centre for Defence Studies, King's College.

Jost, D. (2000) 'The NATO capabilities gap and the European Union', *Survival*, 42, 4.

Missiroli, A. (2002) 'EU–NATO cooperation in crisis management: no Turkish delight for ESDP', *Security Dialogue*, 33, 1, March 2002.

Missiroli, A. (2003a) 'EU enlargement and CFSP/ESDP', *European Integration*, 25, 1.

Missiroli, A. (2003b) 'Ploughshares into swords? Euros for European defence', *European Foreign Affairs Review*, 8, 1.

Missiroli, A. (2003c) *Euros for ESDP: Financing EU Operations*, Paris: EU–ISS Occasional Papers, 45, June.

Missiroli, A. (2003d) 'Turkish delights? A response to Bilgin', *Security Dialogue*, 34, 3.

Quille, G. (2003) 'Making multilateralism effective: the EU Security Strategy', *European Security Review*, Brussels: ISIS Europe, July 2003.

Quille, G., Pullinger, S., Mawdsley, J. *et al.* (2003) *Defence Equipment for European Crisis Management*, European Parliament Working Papers, No. 123, POLI.

Rutten, M. (comp.) (2001) *From St Malo to Nice – European Defence: Core Documents*, Chaillot Paper 47, Paris: EU–ISS.

Schake, K. (2002) *Constructive Duplication: Reducing EU Reliance on US Military Assets*, London: Centre for European Reform.

Further reading

Brimmer, E. (ed.) (2002) *The EU's Search for a Strategic Role*, Washington, DC: Center for Transatlantic Relations.

Chalmer, M. (2002) *Sharing Security: The Political Economy of Burdensharing*, London: Macmillan.

Deighton, A. (2002) 'The European Security and Defence Policy', *Journal of Common Market Studies*, 40, 4.

Duke, S. (2002) *The EU and Crisis Management: Development and Prospects*, Maastricht: EIPA.

Heisbourg, F. *et al.* (2000) *European Defence: Making It Work*, Paris: Chaillot Paper 40, WEU–ISS.

Schmitt, B. (ed.) *European Armaments Cooperation: Core Documents*, Paris: Chaillot Paper 59, EU–ISS.

www.isis-europe.org; www.iss-eu.org

8   The transatlantic dimension

Simon Serfaty

Summary

This chapter reviews US attitudes and policies toward European integration. For much of the Cold War, the United States publicly favoured an ever-closer and ever-larger Europe. The logic was compelling. An integrating Europe helped contain the Soviet Union, and its economic recovery and growing prosperity was advantageous to American business interests. Yet with the fall of the Berlin Wall on 9 November 1989, and most visibly since the horrific events of 11 September 2001, Europe and America have seemed to be moving apart. Now, the American fear is that of a European partner, united and strong, that would act as an adversarial counterweight rather than the genuine, albeit junior, partner that had been envisioned in earlier years. Given such apprehensions, there have been US attempts to play off 'Old' and 'New Europe'. This strategy may bring short-term benefits but could seriously damage European unity and transatlantic solidarity.

Early US support for European integration

The European institutional order promoted by the US after the Second World War was designed to overcome the Westphalian system of nation-states organised on the basis of balance of power. Twice during the first half of the twentieth century, that system had produced global military conflicts that started in Europe but which European states could not end without US military intervention. While US involvement in Europe could not be sustained in 1919 (failure of the US Senate to ratify the League of Nations), it was maintained after 1945 when the Truman administration invested the full range of America's resources, economic, political and military, in western Europe. The western half of the continent was all the more willing to accept America's leadership as it recognised the full scope of its own decline.

The US combined the idea of a united and ultimately stronger Europe with an Atlantic idea that accepted the need for a US commitment to Europe's defence, pending a military recovery that would enable the new allies to share the collective burden of their security. Neither of these ideas was accepted spontaneously, however, and each of them was cause for some concern. President Roosevelt did not like the thought of European unity and he liked even less the prospect of a US entanglement in Europe. As the war was coming to an end, the US president planned instead to withdraw from Europe at the earliest possible time, a message Stalin heard and welcomed at Yalta. Roosevelt also wanted to end Europe's imperial possessions, a message European leaders heard and did not welcome (Harper 1994: 45). After Roosevelt's death in April 1945, however, and in the context of mounting Cold War tensions, a transatlantic consensus gradually emerged around two propositions: an extended US commitment was indispensable, and unity among the states of Europe was desirable. These two propositions were not only compatible but more significantly, they were complementary.

America's major fear was that of another conflict that would start by expansionist design or by *revanchiste* instinct. In other words, keeping Russia out and Germany down also demanded that America be kept in. With the states of Europe painfully aware of the dual threat they could no longer balance on their own, the new European order envisioned by the US was welcomed as the best, but also the only, available option. In April 1949, a year after France and Britain had extended their bilateral anti-German Treaty of Dunkirk with a broader Western European Union (WEU) that responded to American preferences, the US joined Canada and ten European countries to sign a North Atlantic Treaty whose Organization (NATO) became the main security pillar of a new Euro-Atlantic institutional order. American support and engagement in Europe was a vitally important factor in providing the secure environment for the launching of the process of European integration.

During the Cold War, bigger was deemed to be better, meaning that the enlargement of both NATO and the EU was actively encouraged within each institution. For NATO, the grand prize of enlargement was Germany, but the earlier entry of Greece and Turkey in 1952, and the subsequent admission of Spain in 1986, made it possible for the US and its allies to fill geo-strategic gaps without which NATO's mission of deterrence would have been less effective. For the EU, there were also successive enlargements that increased the democratic and affluent space that was spreading throughout western Europe. Thus, there emerged a direct link between the 'ever-closer union' envisioned by the treaty of Rome and the ever-larger security system of the Washington Treaty. Indeed, as long as the Cold War lasted only NATO members found their way into the three enlargements that doubled EU membership between 1958 and 1986. As to NATO, by 1991 only three of its European members were not members of the Union, with two of these (Norway and Iceland) unwilling to accept EU membership.

During the Cold War, adversarial relations were reduced to one country (the Soviet Union) and its communist ideology. Alliance relations, which were not expected to be as entangling as they became, involved many nations with different traditions and many interests that invited tensions and caused conflicts, both across the Atlantic as well as within Europe. Under such conditions, taking the idea of a united Europe seriously was never easy in the United States. Although the idea had been inspired by American history and guaranteed by American policies, the US view of Europe was always ambivalent.

Troubled partnership

The Cold War helped shape and reinforce the rise of a strong and relatively cohesive West. In the US, the threat of Soviet expansion helped the Truman administration to justify what it was probably determined to do in any case. For different reasons, France, the UK and West Germany welcomed the major American commitment to the defence of western Europe. To many Americans, it was natural that Europe would wish to develop along the lines of the US model. In external affairs, American politicians and officials had a decisive say in developing the new liberal international order based on multilateral institutions such as the UN, the International Monetary Fund (IMF), the World Bank and the General Agreement on Tariffs and Trade (GATT), the forerunner of the WTO.

Shortly after the Second World War, Theodore White wrote that

> the American traveler comes to a Europe which is more foreign to Americans today than it has ever been in all our history. This separation of European and American civilizations happens, moreover, at a moment when America is finally more intimately involved in European affairs than ever before in our national history.
>
> (White 1953: 23)

Over the years, however, this cultural gap has been progressively bridged as travellers who crossed the Atlantic with increasing ease and speed ceased to go from one civilisation to another, as it appeared after the war. Now it is more like moving from one family residence to another, with all the attendant family squabbles.

Such intimacy hardly came easily. For one, Americans found the process of integration under way in Europe difficult to follow and comprehend. Even the most sensitive American observers remained frustrated by the slow pace of Europe's integration and puzzled over its erratic evolution. 'The prospect of a European federation,' wrote historian Hajo Holborn (1953: 1), 'has aroused great enthusiasm in the United States, but at the same time the difficulties encountered in its realization have generated a host of frustrations.' Arthur N. Holcombe, in the same year, seemed more patient with the 'many difficulties to be overcome, many conflicting interests to be reconciled', but at the same time he sensed well the new US dilemma. 'The immediate problem of American policy is not to decide whether to support or oppose the further unification of Europe, but rather how far to go in trying to influence the nature and extent of a European Union' (Holcombe 1953: 426–7).

Counterfeit, counterpart and counterweight

Thus emerged the various US attitudes toward Europe, through dramatic events such as German rearmament, the stillborn European Defence Community, the clash over Suez, the French withdrawal from NATO's military command and Kennedy's offer of a new transatlantic partnership. For many sceptical Americans, the idea of a united and strong Europe was dismissed as a *counterfeit,* a dangerous illusion that might prompt a voiceless and powerless Europe to speak and act before its time. But for those who might acknowledge progress, the emergence of a more united and stronger Europe could be both good and bad, depending on whether such unity and strength were used as a *counterpart* of American power. Would Europe be a partner that was able and willing to share America's burdens of leadership, or would it act as a *counterweight* and stand in the way of US leadership in and beyond Europe?

In April 1973, Henry Kissinger's call for a renewed Atlantic consensus was designed to rely on the allies' new weight to compensate for America's declining power. Rather dramatically, Kissinger announced that '1973 is the year of Europe because the era that was shaped by the decisions of a generation ago is ending' (Serfaty 1984: 57). Admittedly, the transatlantic agenda had become somewhat adversarial with currency crises, trade rivalries, competing views of the third world and incompatible expectations in the East. But the bitterness and acrimony caused in Europe by the US proposal, despite the extensive consultation that had reportedly preceded it, reflected a growing vision gap across the Atlantic. Kissinger's true objective, it was argued, was to divide Europe and create a US-dominated Atlantic community, a similar objective to John F. Kennedy's own grand design ten years earlier. More modestly, with Europe pledged to achieve political union by 1980, Kissinger feared that a pre-emptive refusal to consult and act with the US might be made the principle defining Europe's quest for an identity of its own. To this extent, the 'year of Europe' was envisioned as an attempt to identify the new boundaries of legitimate differences between America and its allies and define new mechanisms that would permit consultation as a prerequisite to a new transatlantic consensus for an increasingly global agenda.

US fears of an adversarial Europe were not entirely new. After the Second World War and into the Cold War, there were concerns about the possible implications of European unity and its potential for a 'third force' that might stand aloof from both East and West. In the 1970s, however, these fears grew more intense, not only because of Europe's recovery but also because of the sudden 'passing of American omnipotence' and the surprising 'appeal of French Gaullism', as Ronald Steel first claimed in 1965. Left unchecked, a Gaullist Europe would confirm the end of an Atlantic fantasy as envisaged by the US under conditions of immense power, but now markedly weaker in relation to allies and adversaries alike (Steel 1964: 4–5; Calleo 1987: 3–4).

The end of the Cold War

With the end of the Cold War, images of a European counterweight became less blurred. For one, notwithstanding all past forecasts of impending failures, an ever more united and ever-larger Europe could no longer be ignored when the single market was established, enlargement to 15 was completed, the single currency was adopted and Britain at last acknowledged the irreversible reality of its European identity. Europe, and only Europe, surmised Sam Huntington, even before the collapse of the Berlin Wall, has 'the population, resources, economic strength, technology, and actual and potential military strength to be the pre-eminent power of the 21st century'. Who else? 'The closest thing to an equal that the United States faces at the beginning of the twenty-first century,' added Joseph Nye a decade later, 'is the European Union' (Huntington 1988: 93; Nye 2002: 29).

But to what ends? 'Since the collapse of the Soviet Union, and America's emergence as the sole superpower,' complained Peter Rodman in March 1999, the purpose of European integration has been 'in large part to build a counterweight to what Europe sees as American dominance.' To that extent, Rodman saw Blair's meeting with Jacques Chirac in St Malo a few months earlier as nothing less than a British 'betrayal' of the US. The same potential for anti-American collusion among EU members was seen in much of the neo-conservative thinking that had increasingly questioned Europe's inhibiting influence on the US during the Cold War, and now feared Europe's hostility to America's new bold designs for the post-Cold War order. 'The whole course of European political and economic integration,' noted John Bolton in August 2000, 'has for quite some time been anti-Americanism.' Nor was this argument confined to American neo-conservatives or French neo-Gaullists. 'Whether or not the United States likes it,' wrote Charles Kupchan, 'Europe is becoming a new center of global power. America's sway will shrink accordingly.' Indeed, for Kupchan this was no longer a 'trend' but already a fact: 'by the time the new [NATO] entrants show up at the welcoming ceremony, NATO's lights will be flickering, leaving it up to the European Union to take command of Europe's security' (Rodman 1999a; Bolton 2000: 6; Kupchan 2002: 67–8).

'The concept of counterweight suggests opposition,' remarked Richard Perle at the 2002 trilateral Commission meeting. 'It suggests that you need to function in order somehow to limit, to restrain [the United States]. That's a deep underlying theme in European thinking.' That view is too limited, however. 'I love the EU,' professed columnist Thomas Friedman in the summer of 2001, 'because in this messy world we're living in, two United States are better than one' (*New York Times*, 22 June). Translating common values and interests into common action, whenever values and interests are deemed to be at risk, cannot be the exclusive task of one dominant ally and an *ad hoc* number of faithful followers organised as subsets of willing (even if incapable) participants. 'We remained spectators,' complained Simone de Beauvoir bitterly as she revisited the inter-war years in Europe (de Beauvoir 1962: 16). This is clearly no longer the case. Europe has ambitions of its own and is determined to play a global role, even at times in opposition to the US. As Will Hutton put it, 'this is a particular challenge to Europe', one that seemingly consists in protecting America from its own excesses 'should [there] be no constraint to the exercise of American will' and military power (Hutton 2002: 89).

Ideas of 'reciprocal counterweights' and 'selective counterparts' might be plausible under conditions of relative balance. Under the current conditions of preponderance, however, the idea would demand an inordinate measure of self-restraint for the US and self-confidence for the EU. Seen through American eyes, especially post 11 September 2001, Europe's neglect of military power disqualifies it from being regarded as a serious partner. For many Europeans, however, the US emphasis on military power, even in the aftermath of 11 September 2001, seems so exclusive as to neglect the deeper causes of the threats that the use of force is designed to prevent or pre-empt. Both perspectives reflect different historical experiences: America, which fought all of its foreign wars outside its borders; Europe, which fought most of them inside. Yet, because neither perspective is entirely wrong, neither perspective is entirely right either. Herein lies America's need for Europe, and Europe's need for America.

In short, power is in the hands of the beholder: there is nothing intrinsically wrong about a unipolar world, as some in Europe insist, but there is nothing intrinsically wrong about a multipolar world, as some in the United States seem to assume. A counterweight need not be adversarial and can instead be sufficiently cooperative to act as a counterpart; but a counterpart without weight is of little value, hardly more than a counterfeit.

The US and enlargement

The US preference for a larger Europe has remained a constant feature of America's commitment to a united Europe. Washington has always supported the successive enlargements of the EU, to the west, south and north, and now to the east. For some Americans, it is as if the best in the West was always expected to lie in the 'new' Europe found at the ever-expanding periphery of the European hard core represented by France and Germany.

The US interest in enlargement is readily understandable against the background of the Cold War. Widening the area of affluence and stability in Europe reinforced and expanded the western area of influence and security sponsored by the US against Soviet expansion and communist encroachment. As European institutions grew, local communist parties receded and a centrist political stability settled in an institutional setting within which France and Germany ended their decades of enmity and became the driving force for closer integration. After that, the benefits of integration were brought elsewhere, in Ireland, Greece, Spain and Portugal, all countries where levels of economic prosperity and political stability soon came to exceed anything achieved in the past. Even more importantly, these gains defined a civilian space within which wars ceased to be thinkable. In short, the idea of Europe helped contain Soviet power and caused a retreat of communist ideology. It also helped America feel increasingly at ease with a democratic Europe and be leader of a cohesive West: at the end of the Cold War, nearly all members of the EU were also NATO members.

After the Cold War, the Bush senior and Clinton administrations quickly endorsed the eastward enlargement of the main Euro-Atlantic institutions. That, too, was not a matter of false sentimentalism. Rather, it had to do with concerns that failure to associate the former adversaries with the benefits of the EU (stability and prosperity) and NATO (security and legitimacy) might perpetuate instabilities inherited not only from the Cold War but also from all the European wars that had preceded it. Enlargement would also renew and strengthen the Atlantic faith of the West by bringing into the alliance and the Union countries whose recent experiences had left them sensitive to, and grateful for, US leadership and values. Moreover, an effective eastward enlargement of the EU (and NATO) would also stand in the way of lingering aspirations to build the emerging Union in opposition to the US. In short, no less than during the Cold War, Americans continued to assume that the bigger the western institutions, the better for the US and, therefore, the West as well.

However, the US interest in a dual enlargement of the West was increasingly pointing to an institutional dilemma for Europe. Would the US-dominated NATO drive the new security agenda, or would the EU be able to develop into, at the very least, a regional security actor? The US initially adopted a cautious approach to NATO enlargement, partly to assuage Russian sensitivities and partly because of doubts about the ability of some candidates to assume the obligations of membership. The US backed a limited expansion of just three countries, Poland, Hungary and the Czech Republic in the first phase.

The converging parallelism of the two processes was confirmed when the EU opened negotiations for accession with the new NATO members and remaining candidates (the three Baltic countries, Bulgaria, Romania, Slovakia and Slovenia). While this next phase of NATO enlargement remained dormant during the latter part of the Clinton administration, which seemed to await EU expansion, the events of 11 September 2001 strengthened the rationale and accelerated the US interest in bringing more of Europe into the institutional architecture inherited from the Cold War. In late 2002, therefore, the enlargement processes for both institutions openly converged when the NATO and EU summits, held a few weeks apart, agreed to add seven members to NATO, and an unprecedented ten new members to the EU, including eight that had either joined NATO in 1999 or were scheduled to join in 2004.

With enlargement, the arithmetic of intra-EU and of US–EU relations became more complex. By complicating policy coordination within the EU and within NATO, enlargement could also expose both institutions to the manipulative manoeuvres of larger non-members. With most of the new EU members expected to remain generally committed to a US view of the world, the United States could rely on a full stable of so-called Trojan horses.

Past phases of EU enlargement have been important for US economic interests. Although such enlargements initially were cause for concern and tedious negotiations, they ultimately contributed to the development of an unparalleled commercial area between the United States and the EU, an area that grew dramatically after the Cold War. Yet, although evidence that a stronger Europe would be a more contentious rival and competitor had been mounting over the years, the economic dimensions of EU enlargement to the east did not precipitate much debate in the US. For one, significant economic opportunities were mainly thought to be in Russia rather than in central and eastern Europe. Even under conditions of robust growth, opportunities in the small and rather poor economies of the new EU members seemed to pale in comparison to Russia and, above all, relative to opportunities with current EU members. Moreover, from the standpoint of economic integration, EU enlargement to the east became a fact long before negotiations for accession were completed.

This does not mean that enlargement is not directly relevant to US economic interests. So long as the CEECs are not in the EU, American pressures can be effectively exerted in other multilateral organisations, like the WTO or even the UN, as was seen during the Iraq crisis in 2003; it is when EU membership begins that US influence erodes and may even end. Nor are estimates that eastward enlargement will be the equivalent of adding an economy the size of the Netherlands to an economic area with a population of 380 million and a gross domestic product in excess of 9 trillion euros, either conclusive or even convincing. While the comparison is designed to minimise the significance of the new members' economies, it can be recalled that over most of the 1990s, the Netherlands was the recipient of twice as much US capital as nearby Mexico, notwithstanding the launch of the North Atlantic Free Trade Association (NAFTA). Moreover, the United States has established a strong economic presence in several of the new EU members, especially Poland where Lockheed's application of a so-called Team USA concept for the sale of F-16 jet fighters in December 2002 confirmed America's ability to adopt an integrated approach to competition which European firms cannot yet match.

The US and Wider Europe

In the 1990s, the ghosts sighted in south-eastern Europe came from an earlier time, when a defunct Ottoman Empire and a moribund Habsburg Empire had left nations looking for a state, and states looking for their borders. Under the competing glares of neighbouring great powers, the Balkans became the battleground of choice. In the former Yugoslavia especially, this sort of territorial anarchy was still feared among ethnic groups that vividly remembered their hatreds of the past, as in Bosnia and Kosovo. Yet, such ethnic conflicts seemed both out of place and out of time in a Europe at the close of the twentieth century. They could, therefore, be ended with relative ease, as long as they were not waged within Russia.

Russia's intimacy with Europe was reinforced when enlargement brought the EU and NATO closer to Russian territory. From the start, Russia had been a main feature of NATO enlargement, if only because of an implicit need to accommodate occasional suggestions that it, too, be made a member of NATO, as opposed to a widely held assumption that EU membership was not an option for Russia. After the Cold War, however, a Russian sense of US neglect progressively sharpened Moscow's interest in the EU. In July 2000, a newly elected President Vladimir Putin approved a foreign policy concept of the Russian federation that identified the EU as Russia's second-highest priority, after the Commonwealth of Independent States (CIS) and before the United States and China, and significantly enough, the first 'common strategy' prepared by the EU was centred on Russia.

In 2003, Vladimir Putin, whose soul had seemingly seduced President Bush at the time of their initial meeting in Slovenia in June 2001, found it possible to move closer to Chirac and Schroeder without breaking ranks with Bush, whose intention, after the war in Iraq, was reportedly to 'forgive' Putin while 'ignoring' Schroeder and 'punishing' Chirac. That, however, would perpetuate an unprecedented condition in Europe, as Washington had never before been separated from both France and Germany and Russia had never before been simultaneously associated with its two continental neighbours. According to some, a separate grand bargain with the fallen superpower in search of a mission and an institutional home would have dire consequences for the EU and NATO.

Unfinished vision

For allies who have been so successful together, Americans and Europeans still fail to understand each other well, especially when it seems to matter most. For Americans, their partners' institutional setting is especially puzzling, not only because of the incomprehensible nature of what has taken place to date, but also because the 'finality' of these institutions remains unpredictable, half-written pages of a plot whose conclusions have been barely outlined. Still, a few US assumptions about Europe might influence European expectations about the United States (see Table 8.1).

First, an increasingly united, institutionally coherent and progressively stronger EU is an important US interest if only because the EU is of vital interest to each of its members. Admittedly, it is tempting for the US to use the newer EU members to reinforce the Atlantic personality of the EU, even at the expense of these countries' own EU identity. For the most part, however, that is not a strategy designed to force any country in Europe to choose between its membership in the EU and its alliance with the United States.

Indeed, on most economic matters, including but not limited to trade, the US deals with Europe as a single entity. On foreign policy and security issues, however, dealing with individual EU countries, or *ad hoc* groupings of EU members, is not an American choice imposed at the expense of European unity, but a European choice imposed upon America at the expense of European solidarity. In early 2003, neither Blair/Aznar nor Chirac/Schroeder would have gained majority support within the EU under the revised voting system agreed at Nice. Changing this condition is for the European countries themselves to decide and for the US to influence, if they can. In short, the disintegration of Europe's institutions is not an option for its members, but it is also not a preferred outcome for the US. A central fear on either side of the Atlantic remains a return to an old Europe, divided and weak, rather than progress toward a new Europe, united and strong.

During the Cold War, US policies towards Europe and European integration served American (and European) interests well. The Old and the New World are now linked together as a virtual Euro-Atlantic state

Table 8.1 American assumptions and European expectations

American assumptions	*European expectations*
• Europe remains America's partner of choice and Europe's unity remains a primary goal	• Institutional disintegration is not an option, but final decisions are for Europe to make
• What America does well is usually good for Europe	• What's good for Europe is usually good for America
• The wider Europe the better	• Bigger is better, but too big is bad
• A stronger Europe is not a NATO problem	• Stronger is harder, too weak is dangerous
• Hegemony is not a US vocation	• US cannot rule the world

populated by thousands of American firms in Europe, and European firms in the US, involving over eight million workers producing an output of about \$1,300 billion a year. The debate over the boundaries of permissible differences between the US and Europe begins, therefore, with the recognition of this economic reality. Europe today is more united, more democratic, more prosperous and safer than at any time before. This has also brought significant gains for the US. For these benefits to be enjoyed by Americans and Europeans alike, and spread to others as well, it will require close cooperation between the US and the EU.

The distinctiveness of the Euro-Atlantic couple is also based on a shared approach to life and governance at the local, national and regional levels. During the Cold War, the making of the EU rekindled close affinities between two societies that had grown apart following the birth of the American Republic. After the Cold War, claims of a steadfast societal separation between the two sides of the Atlantic were exaggerated. For the most part, differences between either side of the Atlantic are smaller than with any other part of the world. Indeed, what stands in the way of Europe becoming more European is that it has already become so very American, thus closing a circle that started with Europe as America's past, and seems to be ending with America as Europe's future. Admittedly, levels of European support for, and confidence in, the US dropped dramatically as a result of the crisis over Iraq. Yet, for the most part, Europeans want their partnership with America to remain close, closer than with any other country.

That more independence from the US would also be sought, though without additional defence spending, confirms Europe's exasperation with an American intrusiveness that many find deceptive and self-defeating. Americans, in return, question a European strategy that hopes to limit US power and influence. Complementarity within the Atlantic Alliance, between NATO and the EU and within the EU begins, therefore, with an agreement over what prime minister Blair has called the difference between 'subservience and rivalry'. This is not an argument for a division of labour that implies a rigidity that neither side would welcome for long. There is no single US–European interest nor even a single European interest on all matters, but interests can still be held in common even when they are not evenly shared. Common interests demand an action that can remain united even when related policies are pursued only in parallel. In other words, the US and Europe cannot be expected to take on everything together, but together it must be expected that they can and will attend to everything.

Admittedly, to become a complete security partner, Europe will have to become militarily capable. A strong Europe would be neither a problem for NATO nor a NATO problem. It is instead a problem for the EU and a European problem, one that may remain beyond resolution as long as most of its members (except Britain and to an extent, France) fail to spend more and as long as all of them fail to make the institutional adjustments needed to spend better. Otherwise, the many gaps that separate them from each other, as well as from the US, will continue to widen: capabilities gaps, technology gaps, governance gaps, policy gaps, credibility gaps and much more. In other words, while the crisis in Iraq has confirmed that divisions within the alliance breed divisions within Europe, there cannot be more unity between the US and Europe without more unity within Europe. Achieving the latter is not a US responsibility, even though on occasion the US has been given responsibility for some of the divisions within Europe, either as an instigator or, more frequently, as a target. But beyond military power alone, the toolbox needed for both security and stability must be kept full enough to avoid war, wage it as a matter of last resort, win it at the least possible cost and end it after it has been won.

Whether the US has enough military power to start and win wars on its own terms is not in doubt; but that power alone may not be enough to prevent or even contain these wars. In 2003, after the 'awesome' display of American military capabilities in Iraq, the escalation of violence that followed also revealed the limits of US military power. Because the tools needed to end wars do not 'belong' to the executive branch to the same extent as the tools needed to win them, the US must rely on significant contributions from allies and friends after liberation has been achieved, in order to complete pacification, initiate reconstruction and pursue rehabilit-ation of the state where a regime change has been imposed. Nor can the US attend to these tasks with one European country, or a hand-picked coalition of willing European countries, more effectively than with the institutions to which most European countries belong or hope to join.

To work out the terms of complementarity will not be easy. A shared political will may be lacking to renew, retool and define a new partner-ship for the twenty-first century. For too many Americans, the EU comes up primarily to describe barriers to US exporters, obstacles to US foreign direct investment, unfair competition for US companies, offensive critics of US values and persistent rivals to US interests. In short, the EU is mainly understood as a dirty (French) word, an endeavour primarily designed to challenge the US at the very moment when the Washington faces unprecedented security challenges. But even assuming shared will among Americans and Europeans alike, capabilities may be so far out of balance as to make inter- or co-operability in the military and other areas too difficult. At some point in the future, a mechanism should be adopted that allows more direct consultation between the US and the EU. The rigid US–EU summit process, which usually focuses on commercial disputes, does not satisfy the need for strategic coordination and policy momentum. All in all, the states of Europe should leave less doubt about their intention to build with the US the same intimacy that the US built with its European allies within NATO. The issue is not one of US member-ship in the EU, but one of association, dialogue and cooperation before decisions are reached.

The first six months of 2003 were a wretched period for transatlantic relations. There was a real danger of trade relations being damaged by EU–US splits, prompting business leaders on both sides of the Atlantic to press the politicians to keep a lid on their disputes. Accordingly, both sides were keen to put on a friendly face at the annual transatlantic summit in June. President Bush and his EU counterparts, Romano Prodi and Costa Simitis, representing the Greek presidency, papered over their differences and stressed their agreement on a wide range of issues from extradition of terrorists to starting talks on an 'open skies' accord. As US casualties mounted in Iraq and the scale of the reconstruction effort became apparent, there was also a more conciliatory mood in Washington towards greater UN involvement in that country, something France, Germany and others had pressed for.

Conclusion

'Most history is guessing, and the rest is prejudice,' wrote Will and Ariel Durant in their monumental *Story of Civilization*. There is a lot of guessing in remembering what was achieved and what is yet to be finalised; and there remains some prejudice that reinforces the unfinished vision of an indispensable partnership between North America and the states of Europe, as well as among the states of Europe. Part of that 'prejudice' is the belief that America was not born into the world to become an empire *à l'européenne*, but to end the age of empires, a principle that helped condition the American revolutionary wars. That same prejudice also reinforces the conclusion that notwithstanding the tensions and bitterness that erupted in 2003, the 'West' is alive though ailing, and dynamic, though weary. What is needed, therefore, is more, not less, integration. Among themselves as a mutually shared right of first refusal but also with new associates and partners, the members of the alliance and of the Union should be able to agree on some immediate priorities and certain key principles on how to define and counter these new threats. The ability to do so will determine whether the bold vision of European and transatlantic integration, which drew two parallel paths after the Second World War, and was refined throughout and since the Cold War, can now be completed by the United States and the states of Europe for the twenty-first century.

References

Beauvoir, Simone de (1962) *The Prime of Life*, London: Weidenfeld & Nicolson, p. 16.

Bolton, J. (2000) 'Creating a European security and defence identity: fact or fantasy', *Cato Institute Policy Forum*, 29 August.

Calleo, D.P (1987) *Beyond American Hegemony: The Future of the Western Hegemony*, New York: Basic Books.

Harper, J.L. (1994) *American Visions of Europe*, New York: Cambridge University Press.

Holborn, H. (1953) 'American foreign policy and european integration', *World Politics*, vol. 6, issue 1, October.

Holcombe, A.N. (1953) 'An American view of the American Union', *American Political Science Review*, vol. 47, no. 2.

Huntington, S. (1988–9) 'The U.S. – decline or renewal', *Foreign Affairs,* winter.

Hutton, W. (2002) *The World We're In*, London: Little, Brown.

Kissinger, H. (1965) *Troubled Partnership*, New York: McGraw Hill.

Kupchan, C.A. (2002) *The End of the American Era*, New York: Alfred A. Knopf.

Nye, J. (2002) *The Paradox of American Power. Why the World's Only Superpower Can't Go It Alone*, New York: Oxford University Press.

Rodman, P. (1999a) *Drifting Apart? Trends in US–European Relations*, Washington, DC: The Nixon Center.

Rodman, P. (1999b) Senate Committee on Foreign Relations, Subcommittee on European Affairs, 'NATO and the European Union's Common Foreign, Security and Defence Policies', *Hearings*, March 24, 1999.

Serfaty, S. (ed.) (1984) *The European Finality Debate and Its National Dimensions*, Washington, DC: The CSIS Press.

Steel, R. (1964) *The End of Alliance: America and the Future of Europe*, New York: Viking Press.

White, T.H. (1953) *Fire in the Ashes, Europe in Mid-Century*, New York: William Sloane Associates.

Further reading

Cameron, F. (2002) *US Foreign Policy After the Cold War*, London: Routledge.

Ikenberry, G.J. (2001) *After Victory: Institutions, Strategic Restraint and the Rebuilding of Order After Major Wars*, Princeton, NJ: Princeton University Press.

Kagan, R. (2003) *Of Paradise and Power: America and Europe in the New World Order*, New York: Alfred A. Knopf.

Lindley-French, J. (2002) *Terms of Engagement: The Paradox of American Power and the Transatlantic Dilemma Post-11 September*, Paris, Chaillot Papers, No. 52 (May).

Lundestad, G. (1998) *'Empire' by Integration*, New York: Oxford University Press.

Pew Research Center For The People & The Press (2003) *Views of a Changing World*, June.

Quinlan, J.P (2003) *Drifting Apart or Growing Together? The Primacy of the Transatlantic Economy*, Washington, DC: Centre for Transatlantic Relations.

Reynolds, D. (ed.) (1994) *The Origins of the Cold War in Europe: International Perspectives*, New Haven and London: Yale University Press.

Serfaty, S. (1992) *Taking Europe Seriously*, New York: St Martin's Press.

9 Europe's future

Fraser Cameron

Summary

The widening–deepening debate will not end with the 2004 IGC. As the Union enlarges again in the next decade there will be further pressure for institutional reform. Although a number of the changes proposed in the draft constitutional treaty will not enter into force before 2009, the EU will have five years of operating at 25 (and perhaps two years at 27) before that date. This is likely to be a very difficult period for the Union, partly due to the problems of digesting such a large and diverse number of new members, and partly due to the enormous political, social and economic challenges facing the EU and its member states.

State of the Union

The state of the Union at the end of 2003 is best described as uncertain. On the one hand the EU has been a tremendous success story, integrating former enemies, establishing a single market and a single currency and helping to stabilise its neighbourhood. But it has also failed to match the US in economic growth, connect with its citizens and punch its weight in the world. On the political front there are no leaders with the vision and commitment to European unification that motivated the founding fathers in the 1950s and Helmut Kohl and François Mitterrand displayed in the 1990s. There are some signs, however, of a revival of the Franco-German alliance, which can only be advantageous for further integration. Britain is not regarded as being at the 'heart of Europe' because of its various opt-outs, especially from the euro. Italy has an unpredictable political leadership while Spain is set for change after the departure of José Maria Aznar.

The political landscape of Europe has also changed with the collapse of communism. There is no longer a major left–right ideological cleavage. The mainstream political parties increasingly compete for the centre ground, leaving space for radical, usually right-wing parties, to develop. The defeat of the French socialists by Le Pen in the first round of the 2002 presidential elections is a good example. Far right parties have also gained ground in Italy, Austria, Portugal, Poland and Denmark. The far right has usually campaigned on an anti-EU platform forcing mainstream parties into the defensive as regards European integration. In some countries, such as the UK, a vehemently anti-EU press has also made life difficult for pro-European governments. Eurosceptic parties have also gained ground in the new member states, especially Poland and Estonia. For some, the concept of joining another Union, so soon after escaping from the Soviet Union, raises fears.

On the economic and social side, Europe faces major problems as a result of its poor economic growth in recent years, demographic structure, generous welfare state provisions and inability to push through structural reforms. Often in history the streets of Paris have proved decisive in producing change. In 2003 the streets of the French capital were the venue for a clash of forces on the issue of pension reform. Without a radical shake-up of the pension system in France (and in other EU countries) there will be little or no prospect of long-term growth. The population of the Union is declining, as is the number of people in employment. Consequently it requires a greater effort by today's workers to finance the pensions of those in retirement. The retirees are also living longer, which means a substantial additional charge to the health care budget.

These domestic concerns are reinforced by external concerns about terrorism, weapons of mass destruction and transnational crime, including drug trafficking and illegal immigration. Most Europeans are more worried about these issues than any 'axis of evil'. By general consensus the EU has not been punching its weight in the world. If the IGC accepts the proposals on external affairs in the draft treaty, it should lead to a sounder institutional basis for European foreign and security policy. The key factor, however, will remain the political will of the member states to act together. Another vitally important element will be the transatlantic link and the future direction of US foreign policy.

The political situation

One of the questions posed in the Laeken declaration was

> how to bring citizens closer to the European design and the European institutions, how to organize politics and the European political area in an enlarged Union and how to develop the Union into a stabilizing factor and a model in the new, multipolar world?

This alleged lack of democracy and accountability has long plagued the EU. Indeed, it is often said that if the EU would submit an application to become a member of itself it would certainly be turned down because it does not fulfil the democracy criteria. It was one of the principal tasks of the Convention to remedy this democratic deficit but, as David Allen shows, there was little enthusiasm among the member states to accept the argument that the president of the Commission should be directly elected by the people. If this had been agreed, it would, at a stroke, have dealt with the criticism of lack of democracy, transparency and accountability. Some European leaders lament this absence of a popular culture surrounding the EU although the bureaucrats who run the machinery seem less perturbed. But the absence of popular support for the European venture and the widespread fears of ordinary people about a Union, centralist in nature and with very opaque decision-making structures, will have to be addressed at some stage.

As David Allen points out, there were high expectations for the Convention partly due to the innovative procedure of involving so many interested parties. But it was always an unrealistic hope that the Convention would produce a treaty that would be simple and easy to understand. Indeed it may be an illusion to think that there is some finished model for the EU. Most democratic systems are quite complicated and evolve over time. Two examples are the devolution process in the UK, with a new parliament for Scotland and assemblies for Wales and Northern Ireland, and the break-up of Czechoslovakia into two separate states in 1993. Furthermore, the transnational nature of European governance is highly complex, especially as most policy areas are in the economic and technical domains.

When criticisms are made that the EU lacks a common public space and demos, unfair comparisons with the US are often made. The 13 American colonies had their differences but they spoke a common language and had a common culture. Europeans speak different languages, watch different TV stations, read different books and newspapers. The elites may be debating Europe's future from the same script but the people are not. European integration has always been an elite-driven process and this is unlikely to change given the complexity of issues discussed and decided at the EU level.

At the same time, the process of integration has brought about a growing European identity. There is considerable evidence that identities are increasingly multiple in today's Europe. Indeed, the primary cleavage is between those who identify only with their nation-state and those who combine national and European identification in various ways, e.g. Cork, Ireland, Europe or Bavaria, Germany, Europe. Gradually a transnational political space is being created. But to make it really effective there needs to be greater multilingualism, more effective cross-national political parties, more informative media and a greater commitment to educational openness.

The EU's political system has been built on endless compromises. This partly reflects the fact that there is no unitary system among member states. There is no universally accepted single paradigm which means that the EU is a *sui generis* structure. Although the Convention and IGC are the formal way forward for the EU, it is important not to neglect evolution.

Leadership is an important factor, as can be seen from a comparison of Delors and Santer, the two Commission presidents prior to Prodi. The standing and efficiency of institutions is also important. For example, the Commission seized the opportunity presented to it in 1989 (by George Bush Senior at the Paris G7 summit) to play the lead role in managing the technical assistance programmes for central and eastern Europe. This gave it control of a large budget and considerable experience in assisting the transformation of states from authoritarianism to democratic structures.

New kids on the block

As Graham Avery points out, EU policies towards the CEECs helped bring the two halves of Europe closer together even before the enlargement negotiations were formally completed. The negotiations provided a valuable learning experience about the EU as did the Convention. Nevertheless, it will not be easy for ten new countries with no experience of the community system to adapt to the EU decision-making structures. There is also a danger that the best and brightest officials from the CEECs will be drawn to work in Brussels because of the high salaries on offer. A mid-level EU official earns more than the prime minister of any new member state.

There is a broad consensus that enlargement must not be allowed to weaken the degree of integration already achieved. In other words, widening and deepening should be pursued simultaneously in order that the Union can continue to act effectively, consistently and in solidarity. The truth is that having encouraged the new member states to make maximum efforts to prepare for membership, the Union has not put the same effort into preparing itself for enlargement, especially in the crucial area of institutional reform. The decisions at Nice and the Convention's draft treaty can only be described as the minimum requirements for an enlarged Union to function.

During the Convention it was difficult to distinguish speakers coming from existing or future member states. Alojz Peterle, who represented the new members in the Presidium, told the author that their lack of EU experience meant that they approached the question of institutional changes with an open mind. With the end of accession negotiations, they became more vocal in their views, with most accepting the importance of the Community system in protecting the rights of smaller and medium-sized members. As Heather Grabbe points out there is no reason to expect that the CEECs will form a bloc in the enlarged Union. They will be as different in their approaches as present member states, forming *ad hoc* alliances on various issues. Enlargement will also have a huge impact on the political culture and the organisation of the Union and its institutions. Assessments of the attitudes of future member states towards closer integration vary. According to some, the candidates would appear to share the same mix of views as the current member states. According to others, the newcomers have neither any understanding nor interest in the community method. Whatever their attitudes when members, there is no doubt that it will take the Union some considerable time to digest such a large number of new member states. Making deals between 25 or more member states will inevitably become more demanding. The intimacy of small meetings will disappear and the linguistic regimes of an enlarged Union almost defy the imagination. In the areas where unanimity is preserved, such as taxation, immigration, CFSP, there are doubts whether effective policy making will be possible with 25 potential vetoes around the table.

The importance of the community system

The success of the enlarged Union will be greatly eased by promotion of the community system for taking decisions. Throughout the history of European integration the community method has permitted the harmonious cooperation of big and small countries. Indeed the extraordinary success of the integration model has been to reassure the smaller countries that their interests will not be over-ridden by their bigger neighbours, without frustrating the interests of the latter. This success has been based on a unique balance between the institutions where the smaller states traditionally have been over-represented.

If one looks at trade policy as a successful example of the community system in operation, three factors stand out. First, the political will to act together. There has been a clear transfer of responsibility for trade policy to the EU level. This sharing of sovereignty did not happen overnight and is not universal. The custom union and the single market were created in stages. Although power to conclude agreements with non-member countries has largely passed to the EU, important aspects such as customs administration, export promotion and bilateral investments remain in the hands of the member states. In other words, there is a functional division of tasks between the EU and member states in line with the principle of subsidiarity that operates to the satisfaction of all concerned.

Second, there is the clear allocation of responsibility in decision-making. The Commission negotiates on behalf of the member states but they retain full political control. The Commission needs both a Council mandate to begin negotiations and its agreement to approve the results. Third, there is a consensus about policy. The more protectionist inclined member states acknowledge that trade liberalisation is crucial to growth and competitiveness while the liberal wing recognises that there is a need for a regulatory framework to take account of social and environmental issues. The extra ingredient is trust, something that only develops over time.

With the admission of several, smaller, new member states, there were fears in the Convention that the balance might tilt too strongly against the larger member states. The balance between big and small states is likely to remain a sensitive issue. The idea that all states are equal is, of course, a myth in the global as well as the EU system. Indeed, from the very start of European integration, the larger member states were given two Commissioners and more votes than the smaller ones. The big–small issue was never a significant problem in the past. Since Nice, and with the growing powers wielded by the EU, it has become an important issue.

Although, as Jean Monnet argued 'nothing can be achieved without institutions', and although the community method has a proven track record, the vital ingredient is the political will of member states to move further down the integration path. The problem is that member states have very different aspirations and ambitions in Europe and for Europe. At present not all member states want to join the euro. Those which have joined the single currency do not all subscribe to the idea of a zone of total economic integration which extends into certain fiscal and social areas. Not all member states have signed the Schengen agreement. Not all member states share the same views on asylum and immigration. Not all member states belong to NATO or share the same views on defence arrangements within the EU. There are sharply differing views on the future institutional balance. After enlargement these differences will inevitably increase and further complicate the future governance of the EU.

For some the solution is a multi-speed Europe. Under pressure of enlargement the EU will be faced with erosion or further integration. If not all member states were willing to move ahead then an avant-garde might take the lead in pushing for further integration. Certainly there will be more opportunities for enhanced cooperation in the future as a result of the proposals in the draft constitutional treaty.

The economic situation

The EU faces a serious economic situation. Globally, the prospects for growth are not good, while at home the member states have fallen behind their declared aims in the Lisbon agenda of the EU becoming the most competitive and dynamic knowledge-based economy in the world. As Andrew Scott points out, so far these high-minded words have not been accompanied by the structural reforms needed for stable growth in the long term.

For several decades, Germany was the 'locomotive' of the European economy. But its public finances were severely strained by the costs of unification and its labour market has proved one of the most inflexible in the EU. Faced with high wage costs, an ageing work force and rising health care provisions, Germany faces a troubled future. A key issue will be the future of the Stability and Growth Pact, which imposes budgetary discipline on the members of the eurozone. Several politicians have called for a loosening of the Pact's tight constraints arguing that while it was necessary to set very strict rules, including independence for the ECB, to ensure the success of the euro's introduction, these strict rules hinder efforts to stimulate the economy. Others argue that the real problem is the failure of national governments to push through structural reforms. Whatever the merits of each argument, the Union will only be seen as successful by its citizens if it contributes to creating a dynamic economy in which higher productivity goes along with significant job creation.

A report by a high-level study group in July 2003 called for a radical change in the Union's economic and budgetary priorities. It argued that while macroeconomic stability had improved in the 1990s and progress had been made on preserving cohesion, the EU had failed to deliver on growth. This underperformance was striking because it contrasts not only with expectations but also with past performance and recent US achievements. Per capita GDP has stagnated at about 70 per cent of the US level since the early 1990s. Growth has to become the top priority to help integrate the new member states and contribute to a more dynamic Union. A more dynamic EU would be a better partner for the Wider Europe and allow it to assume greater global responsibilities.

The report went on to argue that sustainability was under threat from rapid developments in demography, technology and globalisation, all of which increase the demand for social protection. In a stark warning, the report stated that failure to deliver on the Lisbon agenda would endanger the whole process of European integration. It suggested that there needed to be a massive and urgent change towards an innovation-based economy in Europe. It called for completion of the single market and making it more dynamic; boosting investment in knowledge; improving the economic governance of the Union; more effective decision-taking and regulation; and refocusing of the budget. This latter recommendation caused considerable controversy as it proposed diverting money spent on agriculture and structural funds towards education, training, science and R&D (Sapir 2003).

As Andrew Scott notes, the new member states will take many years to catch up with current members assuming continuing high levels of growth. But if these growth rates do not materialise it could lead to serious political, economic and social consequences. The expectations of populations in central Europe are high. Many believe that massive EU financial transfers will immediately improve their daily lives and that they may delegate solutions of all their considerable domestic problems to the EU. Chief among these problems is agricultural reform. The agricultural populations of Poland and Romania are larger than the entire agricultural workforce in the present EU. The Commission calculates that applying the CAP, even partially, to the new member states will cost the farm budget nearly four billion euros by 2006. There will be 15 million farmers, all dependent on subsidies from Brussels, in the EU of 27 member states. Enlargement will thus increase the political weight of countries that have an expansionary view of the EU budget. How will this affect the struggle to refocus the EU budget on the 'innovative economy'?

Heather Grabbe suggests that there might be different short- and long-term aims for the CEECs. In the short term, those countries heavily dependent on agriculture will seek increased agricultural support; all will seek increased access to the structural funds. These financial transfers should help stimulate economic growth as they did with regard to Spain, Portugal, Greece and Ireland. At the same time 2003 was a difficult year for the CEECs, with growth slowing and reforms stalling. The multiple strains of preparing for EU membership are particularly visible in the largest four countries, Poland, Hungary, the Czech Republic and Slovakia. The main problem is rising budget deficits. Governments are trying to impose painful cuts but all four states are far from their eventual target, the 3 per cent limit set by the TEU for the eurozone.

Hopes that rapid economic growth would reduce deficits by generating extra tax revenues have repeatedly been dashed. The GDP increases of 5 per cent plus recorded in the 1990s are a distant memory. Most CEECs will find it hard to reach 3 per cent in 2003–4. Although this compares well with the eurozone, the CEECs are starting from a much lower base. In addition, their economies are burdened with excess bureaucracy, loss-making state-owned industries and communist-era welfare schemes. Voters are becoming tired of 'blood, sweat and tears' exhortations by political leaders and many who have lost out (public service workers, farmers, pensioners, unemployed) are turning to support radical, nationalist, political parties. This could be lead to a sizeable group of eurosceptics in the new member states.

The budget issue will also become the focus of a fierce struggle soon after enlargement. Germany has made clear that it will no longer play the role of 'paymaster' of the EU and has called for an end to the British rebate (a mechanism agreed in 1984 to compensate the UK for its high net contributions because it does not benefit so much from CAP payments). France has traditionally resisted substantial cuts in the CAP. Spain has equally resisted efforts to trim the structural funds. But how long can this resistance continue in the face of poor rates of economic growth and lack of structural reform? A related issue is whether the ceiling of 1.27 per cent of EU GDP can be sustained in light of new priorities. Should the Union not be able to raise its own taxes? Taxes are unpopular but the constant wrangles over contributions to the EU budget also damage the Union. It should not be too difficult to devise a transparent and efficient system for collecting some revenue that would merit the name 'own resources'. These issues are likely to be at the fore of public debate in the coming years.

Europe's future borders

As Geoffrey Harris points out there is a Europe beyond the EU and no discussion of the widening–deepening debate can avoid reference to the impact of enlargement and the EU's new borders on the Wider Europe.

There is little advantage in trying to define the final border of the Union at this stage. To the north, only Norway, Iceland and Greenland remain outside the Union. To the west, Ireland forms a clear frontier. To the south, islands in the Mediterranean have been judged eligible for membership but not countries such as Morocco on the North African mainland. To the east, the geographic border of Europe lies at the Ural mountains but the Urals are not even an internal border of the Russian Federation. Although Berlusconi is a strong advocate of Russian membership of the EU, it is difficult to imagine Russia ever joining, not least because of its size and world power pretensions. President Yeltsin once called for his country to join the EU but no such aim has been heard from Mr Putin, his successor. There is little doubt, however, that after enlargement there will be a greater emphasis on relations with the new neighbours in the east, south-east and south.

In the east, Ukraine is the most important country, as big as France in size and population. It has declared that its medium-term aim is membership of the EU but its economic problems would seem to preclude any prospect of membership of the Union in the foreseeable future. Moldova and Belarus are, for different reasons, 'failed states' but the EU will inevitably have to become more involved with both countries. The EU will similarly have to become more engaged in the Caucasus. In south-east Europe, Romania and Bulgaria have a target date of 2007 for EU membership. Croatia, which applied in February 2003, also hopes to join on this date while other western Balkan countries hope to join in the next decade. Others, including Norway (again), and Switzerland after the successful UN referendum in March 2002, may follow, which demonstrates the impossibility of drawing hard and fast lines now as to who should or should not be considered as future members of the Union.

A key country is Turkey, which applied for EU membership fifteen years ago. The European Commission is due to make a report by December 2004 on whether Turkey fulfils the criteria to open accession negotiations. Polls show a vast majority of EU citizens against Turkish membership and indeed many are worried about the impact of the current enlargement on their jobs and living standards. The next enlargement, to include the 33 million poor citizens of Bulgaria and Romania in 2007, will further strain the solidarity of EU citizens and governments. Turkey will probably require another decade to prepare for membership. It will have to improve its democratic credentials, implement economic and juridical reforms and demonstrate a constructive approach to the Cyprus issue.

Although ineligible for membership, the Mediterranean countries of the North African littoral also wish to develop closer relations with the Union. As Geoffrey Harris notes, so far the Barcelona process has been a disappointment. The EU has put large sums of money into the countries of the region but has failed to open its markets to their agricultural exports. The countries of the region have paid mere lip service to reform. It remains to be seen whether the EU will be serious about its proposals to introduce more conditionality into its relations with its southern partners.

Security

For over half a century the US has provided Europe with a security guarantee. But how long will this continue? Antonio Missiroli and Gerrard Quille point to the slow but steady development of CFSP and ESDP, with the first EU peacekeeping missions taking place in 2003. Many Americans, however, might question why the US still retains a sizeable military presence in Europe when Europe has a bigger population than the US, a comparable GDP, more men in uniform and faces no real military threat. Europeans might ask themselves whether it was not time that Europe was able to look after its own security. The security situation in Europe is certainly in a state of flux. What will be the future role of NATO? How quickly will the EU develop increased military capabilities? Will enlargement help or hinder the EU's ambitions in CFSP and ESDP? How much money will be available for defence given the tightened economic situation?

One of the principal aims of the Convention was to produce a framework for the Union to play a more assertive role on the world stage, a role commensurate with its economic strength. Sadly the debates on this matter in the Convention were overshadowed by the EU's disarray over the Iraq crisis. It seemed to many that the EU's global ambitions could be put back in cold storage when the major players were in such open disagreement on a central security issue. But such was the shock of the Iraq crisis on the European body politic that member states resolved to try and overcome their differences. One consequence was the mandate given by the European Council to Mr Solana to prepare the first-ever European security strategy. This paper, presented to European leaders in June, highlighted the threats from international terrorism, weapons of mass destruction and proliferation. It urged the EU to take a robust attitude in tackling these threats while simultaneously arguing for a more effective multilateral system. After years of hesitation and disagreement, the Union now has the makings of an agreed strategic concept. This is quite some progress.

Europe in the world

Over the years, the Union has gradually become an increasingly important global actor. Surely, it is quite a different actor to the US but this is a result mainly of bringing together the external policies of 15 member states with very different experiences, traditions and capabilities. The Union has developed common policies in a number of difficult areas, from the Balkans and the Middle East to North Korea and Russia. Bilateral diplomacy continues but the member states increasingly recognise that an EU of 15/25 members is far more effective in influencing third countries than acting alone. One of the interesting proposals in the Convention was that for an EU diplomatic service, which would be based on the existing Commission delegations and be staffed by EU officials and member state diplomats. The Solana paper drew attention to the huge number of diplomats working for the member states and questioned whether there might not be scope for greater sharing. As financial pressures continue to bite, it is likely that member states will see the merit of moving down this path.

Another key relationship is that with the US. As Simon Serfaty notes, the US has always had an ambivalent attitude towards European integration. For half a century it has supported moves for a closer Union, despite occasional disputes. Since the end of the Cold War, however, the glue that held the transatlantic relationship together has weakened. As the EU has become more coherent and assertive it has increasingly taken different positions from the US, on issues ranging from global warming, the ICC, support for multilateralism to genetically modified foods. One of the biggest disputes was over the Iraq war in the spring of 2003, which also caused splits within the EU. These developments have led some US politicians to question whether a more integrated Europe is really in America's best interests. Mr Rumsfeld put it bluntly when he talked of 'new Europe' being friendlier towards America then 'old Europe'. Such views are short-sighted. The EU may develop into an occasionally prickly partner of the US but it will remain the most important partner for the US. Given the 'soft power' that the EU brings to the table in terms of political, economic, financial and cultural assets, plus a developing military capability, Washington will find it impossible to ignore the EU. The bottom line is that when the EU and US work together, they get things done; when they oppose each other, nothing is achieved. But the EU will have to learn to speak and act together in a more coherent manner. As Simon Serfaty rightly concludes, 'there cannot be more unity between the US and Europe without more unity within Europe'.

A research agenda

This book has demonstrated that there are many important challenges facing the enlarged EU. For the student a number of interesting research terms may be identified. On the political front it will be important to analyse the impact of the IGC treaty changes on the functioning of the Union. How will the structures created for a Community of six cope with enlargement? How will political development within the member states affect the prospects of integration? Will euroscepticism continue to be a politically significant factor? On the social and economic side, it will be important to monitor progress on the Lisbon agenda and consider the implications of reforms, especially pensions, to the welfare state. Is Europe likely to follow the Anglo-Saxon model, the Scandinavian, the Rhineland or what? The budget debate of 2004–6 will be another fascinating area to observe as national and community interests compete for funding. Another important social issue will be immigration. The EU needs immigrants for economic reasons but generally speaking immigrants face problems of discrimination. How to create a stable, tolerant, multicultural society will be a major challenge for Europe. On the global front the EU will have to define its strategic interests. What are the common interests of an EU stretching from Ireland to Estonia, from Sweden to Cyprus? How will the Union articulate and defend its interests on the world stage?

Conclusion

The questions on the table at the Convention were not whether the Union should adopt major new areas of competence, as all the big projects required to construct a political union (single market, single currency, foreign and defence policy, justice and home affairs) are already *in situ* or under way. Rather the EU has to cope with its own success and explain to its citizens the nature of the EU system, tackle the questions of account-ability and legitimacy and institutional reform. It is national leaders who must bear most of the responsibility for the failures in these fields. By and large they have neglected to 'sell Europe' at home. When things go wrong, the tendency is to blame Brussels; when there are successes they take the credit, never Brussels.

During the Convention the traditional divisions between those favouring the community method and those preferring the intergovernmental path were again exposed. The final destination of the European integration process has always been a matter of contention. The differences between those favouring a federal European state and those favouring a looser construction with the emphasis on the nation-state have been successfully camouflaged for several decades. This ambiguity has arguably served Europe well as it has been the only way to maintain a minimum consensus amidst conflicting agendas concerning the scope, speed and the very nature of the integration process. For example, there is no realistic prospect of environmental policy being shifted to intergovernmentalism, or of defence policy being shifted to the community pillar in the foreseeable future. There is, however, a serious prospect of moving some policy issues in JHA from the intergovernmental to the community system.

The fundamental question is how to ensure that an enlarged EU of 25 or more member states continues to function on the basis of democracy, transparency and efficiency. States join the Union because it gives them added value. It increases their influence and provides a greater opportunity to achieve their policy aims or, to put it another way, it increases their real sovereignty that has gradually been lost through globalisation. But if member states consider that they no longer receive any real benefit from the Union, perhaps because of paralysis of decision-making in an enlarged Union, or that the voting system has become seriously inequitable, then some members might ask why bother to stay in the club. One thing is sure, however, the widening–deepening debate will continue for many years to come.

References

Sapir, A. (2003) 'An agenda for a growing Europe'. http://www.europa.eu.int/comm/commissioners/prodi/pdf/agenda_for_growing_europe_en.pdf.

Appendix

The new members

	Population, millions	GDP per head, % of EU average at PPP	% of people working in agriculture
Bulgaria	7.9	28	27
Cyprus	0.8	80	5
Czech Republic	10.2	57	5
Estonia	1.4	42	7
Hungary	10.2	51	6
Latvia	2.4	33	15
Lithuania	3.5	38	17
Malta	0.4	55*	2
Poland	38.6	40	19
Romania	22.4	25	44
Slovakia	5.4	48	6
Slovenia	2.0	69	10
Turkey	68.6	22	35
EU	377.5	100	4

Sources: European Commission; Eurostat from national sources.

Notes:

Data from 2002. *Data for Malta from 1999.

PPP means purchasing power parity, a measure of the exchange rate that corrects for misalignments in foreign exchange markets.

Glossary

The **Community system** refers to the way in which decisions are taken under shared sovereignty. The Commission proposes new laws and the EP and Council decide together on whether to accept them. In many areas these decisions can be taken by QMV. This system is often described as supranational.

The **democratic deficit** is the term used to describe the alleged lack of parliamentary oversight of the EU institutions. It also covers the inability of the citizens to directly elect either the president of the Council or the president of the Commission.

Enhanced cooperation is one of several similar terms (structured cooperation, multi-speed Europe, hard core, avant garde) allowing some member states to move ahead faster than others towards closer integration.

The **eurozone** is composed of those member states using the euro as their currency.

Federalism refers to a system of government where decisions are taken at different levels. The US and Germany are examples of federal systems. Increasingly, the UK is a federal system with the creation of a Scottish parliament and a Welsh assembly. But the word 'federal' has become associated in the UK and some other countries with increasing powers for the EU institutions. Originally in the draft constitution it was dropped under pressure from the UK.

An **intergovernmental conference (IGC)** is made up of the heads of state or government of all the member states (plus the Commission as a non-voting member) or their representatives to negotiate changes to the treaties.

The **intergovernmental system** refers to decisions taken by governments under the rule of unanimity. Every country has a veto. This applies to areas such as taxation and defence.

Schengen is a small town in Luxembourg where member states agreed to cooperate closer in some JHA areas such as passport controls. The UK has an 'opt-out' of Schengen.

An **'opt-out'** means that some member states have negotiated or been granted permission not to apply some parts of the treaty. The UK negotiated an 'opt-out' of the single currency (euro) and the Social Chapter at Maastricht. Denmark negotiated 'opt-outs' of defence policy and some JHA areas after its failed referendum in 1992.

Sovereignty generally refers to the exercise of power. Nation-states are traditionally the political entity that exercises power. But in the EU, sovereignty is often shared between the member states and the institutions. Many argue that in today's world of globalisation it is impossible for any one nation-state to exercise complete sovereignty. The EU is unique in that it is the only political system that seeks to pool sovereignty for the greater good of its members.

Subsidiarity in the European context means taking decisions at the national or regional as opposed to the EU level.

Index